RESTORATIVE JUSTICE
AND
JESUS

Dr. Maxwell Shimba

Shimba Publishing LLC
Printed in the United States of America

First Printing Edition, 2023
ISBN: 9798873482078

TABLE OF CONTENTS

PREFACE

In the pursuit of justice, humanity has navigated a spectrum of approaches, from punitive measures to more transformative, healing-centered paradigms. Within this spectrum, the lens of Jesus' teachings casts a unique and compelling light on the concept of justice—specifically, through the transformative philosophy known as restorative justice.

This book delves into the profound intersection of restorative justice and the teachings of Jesus, exploring the harmonies between the principles embedded in the Gospels and the transformative processes that define restorative justice. As we embark on this exploration, we are invited to consider justice not merely as an abstract concept but as a lived experience, intricately woven into the fabric of our relationships, communities, and broader society.

Restorative justice, with its emphasis on healing, reconciliation, and community engagement, finds resonance with the ethos of Jesus' ministry. The parables, actions, and teachings of Jesus illuminate pathways to address harm, seek forgiveness, and restore broken relationships—core tenets that align seamlessly with the restorative justice framework.

As we journey through the pages of this book, we will encounter the teachings of Jesus on justice, the application of restorative principles in diverse contexts, and the challenges and promises that lie on the path of embracing restorative justice through the lens of Jesus. Each chapter unfolds a facet of this exploration, weaving together theological insights, practical applications, and real-world case studies.

This work is not just an academic exercise; it is a call to reflect on how we, as individuals and communities, can embody the principles of restorative justice in our quest for justice. It beckons us to consider the potential of a justice system rooted in love, compassion, and the transformative power of forgiveness.

May this exploration inspire conversations, spark transformative actions, and contribute to a broader dialogue on justice—one that draws from the wellspring of wisdom found in the teachings of Jesus and the profound potential of restorative justice. As we delve into these pages, let us embark on a journey that transcends theoretical frameworks and touches the heart of what it means to seek justice with empathy, compassion, and the spirit of reconciliation.

Dr. Maxwell Shimba
President
Shimba Institute for Restorative Justice

INTRODUCTION

In the quest for justice, humanity has grappled with diverse approaches—ranging from retribution to restoration—each seeking to address harm, wrongdoing, and conflict within the intricate tapestry of society. At the heart of this exploration lies a profound intersection between the teachings of Jesus and the philosophy of restorative justice. This book embarks on a transformative journey, unraveling the threads that weave these two realms together, inviting readers to ponder the depths of justice through the lens of compassion, reconciliation, and redemption.

Restorative justice, as a paradigm, emerges not as a departure from punitive measures but as a radical reimagining of justice—a vision grounded in the transformative teachings encapsulated in the Gospels. As we navigate through the pages that follow, we traverse the terrain of theological insights, practical applications, and poignant case studies that illuminate the pathways to a justice that heals, reconciles, and restores.

The chapters within this book unfold organically, each exploring a facet of the profound connection between restorative justice and the teachings of Jesus. From understanding the theological underpinnings of justice in the Gospels to delving into real-world applications, challenges, and promises, this exploration invites readers into a contemplative space where justice is not a distant ideal but a lived experience woven into the fabric of our shared humanity.

We encounter the parables of Jesus as timeless narratives that speak to the core of restorative justice principles—stories that echo through the corridors of time, resonating with the potential for transformation and redemption. Real-world case studies illustrate how these principles manifest in various contexts, from criminal justice systems to schools, families, and communities.

This book is not a mere academic exercise; it is a call to action. It invites readers to reflect on their understanding of justice, encouraging a shift from punitive instincts toward an embrace of healing-centered justice. As we explore the pages that follow, we are asked not only to contemplate but to embody the principles of restorative justice in our individual lives, communities, and broader societal structures.

May this journey through the intersection of restorative justice and the teachings of Jesus inspire a renewed vision for justice—one that is compassionate, empathetic, and grounded in the transformative power of forgiveness. We hope that this exploration contributes to a broader conversation, inviting individuals, communities, and societies to consider the potential of justice that echoes the profound love and compassion exemplified by Jesus.

DR. MAXWELL SHIMBA

CHAPTER 01

UNDERSTANDING RESTORATIVE JUSTICE

Restorative justice is a profound and transformative approach to addressing harm and conflict in society. At its core, it seeks to restore relationships, promote healing, and reintegrate individuals who have caused harm back into their communities. Unlike traditional punitive justice, which often focuses on punishment and isolation, restorative justice offers a more holistic and empathetic perspective.

Restorative justice places a significant emphasis on the needs of victims, recognizing that they have been directly affected by the harm caused. It provides them with a platform to express their feelings, seek answers, and have a say in how the offender can make amends. This victim-centered approach is a fundamental principle of restorative justice, and it acknowledges the importance of their emotional and psychological recovery.

Moreover, restorative justice involves holding the offender accountable for their actions. However, the accountability process is not punitive but rather restorative in nature. Offenders are encouraged to take responsibility for their actions, understand the harm they've caused, and actively participate in making amends. This process can involve apologies, restitution, community service, or other actions aimed at repairing the harm done.

Restorative justice also extends its reach beyond the immediate parties involved in a conflict. It emphasizes the broader community's role in facilitating healing and reconciliation. Communities play an active role in supporting both victims and offenders in their journey towards resolution. This aspect creates a sense of shared responsibility and collective healing.

Restorative practices often involve facilitated discussions in ternary varieties: Victim Offender Mediation, family group conferences, and circle processes. Victim Offender Mediation is the most widely used method within restorative practices and has been shown to provide high rates of satisfaction among all parties. Apostle Paul used these techniques by making Onesimus, Philemon, and the Church to meet and resolve the issues between Onesimus and Philemon – Philemon Chapter 1 Verse 10-14. 10 I beseech thee for my son Onesimus, whom I have begotten in my bonds: 11which in time past was to thee unprofitable, but now profitable to thee and to me: 12 whom I have sent again: thou therefore receive him, that is, mine own bowels: 13 whom I would have retained with me, that in thy stead he might have ministered unto me in the bonds of the gospel: 14but without thy mind would I do nothing; that thy benefit should not be as it were of necessity, but willingly.

Paul announces his intention to send Onesimus directly back to Philemon and describes Onesimus as his very own affections, which expresses his deep personal love and affection for Philemon's runaway slave.

This description would serve to further soften the blow of coming into contact with Onesimus and serve to bring about a reconciliation between the two and assuage any anger Philemon might have towards his slave. Romans 12:10. Be devoted to one another in love.

Honor one another above yourselves

Victim Offender Mediation differs from traditional mediation in that "mediation does not presume a harm causing party and a harmed party," while Victim Offender Mediation and other restorative justice methods are in fact predicated on the harm caused to one party by another party. Restorative conferences should be combined with other restorative practices to create an appropriate plan to heal and re store each party to an offense.

Therefore, Victim Offender Mediation process or proceedings for resolving crime (an action or omission that constitutes an offense that may be prosecuted by the state and is punishable by law) by focusing on redressing the harm done to the victims, holding offenders accountable for their actions and, often also, engaging the community in the resolution of that conflict is called "restorative justice".

Participation of the parties is an essential part of the process that emphasizes relationship building, reconciliation, and the development of agreements around a desired outcome between victims and offender. Restorative justice processes can be adapted to various cultural contexts and the needs of different communities. Through them, the victim, the offender, and the community regain some control over the process. Furthermore, the process itself can often transform the relationships between the community and the justice system as a whole.

Micah 6:8 He has shown you, O man, what is good. And what does the LORD require of you? To act justly to love mercy and to walk humbly with your God. (New International Version)

God is expecting us to act justly, which raises the questions, "What is justice", and "What does it mean to act justly?" These are some of the questions we will explore in this book.

While justice can be used to talk about retributive justice in which a person is punished for their wrongdoings, most of the time the Bible uses the word justice to refer to restorative justice, in which those who are unrightfully hurt or wronged are restored and given back what was taken from them as it is impeccable exhibited in the Book of Philemon- Read my Book – Runaway Slave.

Restorative justice is an approach to understanding and responding to crime. In terms of understanding crime, restorative justice theory emphasizes crime as harm to people, relationships, and communities. In terms of responding to crime, restorative justice practice focuses on repairing the harm inflicted by crime on people, relationships, and communities, and on giving those directly affected by the crime the opportunity to determine what that repair will look like.

Restorative justice practices incorporate several key principles or values;

Encounter – those involved in and affected by a crime should have opportunity to encounter or engage each other personally in response to it;

Inclusion – all of those involved in and affected by a crime should be included in the response, to it to the extent they want to be involved;

Amends – an offender should have opportunity to make amends, symbolical and material, for the harm caused by his or her actions; and

Reintegration – the response to a crime should seek full integration of the offender and the victim into their communities.

In its fullest and best sense, restorative justice is a binary way of seeing crime correctly and a way of responding to crime appropriately.

In the studies which follow, we will have opportunity to explore carefully the meaning and practice of restorative justice. In faith, hope, and love, may we ask God for grace to grow so that at the end of the week, and beyond, we can do better what God requires of us to act justly, to love mercy, and to walk humbly with him.

Isaiah 32:16-20

Justice will dwell in the desert and righteousness live in the fertile field.

The fruit of righteousness will be peace; the effect of righteousness will be quietness and confidence forever.

My people will live in peaceful dwelling places, in secure homes, in undisturbed places of rest.

Though hail flattens the forest and the city is leveled completely, how blessed you will be, sowing your seed by every stream, and letting your cattle and donkeys' range free. (New International Version)

Hosea 2:18-20

In that day I will make a covenant for them with the beasts of the field and the birds of the air and the creatures that move along the ground.

Bow and sword and battle I will abolish from the land, so that all may lie down in safety.

I will betroth you to me forever; I will betroth you in righteous- ness and justice, in love and compassion.

I will betroth you in faithfulness, and you will acknowledge the Lord.

(New International Version)

Reflection on justice:

In the passages from Isaiah and Hosea we see a picture of justice. Rich in imagery and meaning, the passages piece together a mosaic of justice using terms such as peace, security, rest, confidence, love, compassion, commitment, faithfulness, and fruitfulness. Justice is connected with right relationships among people and in all of creation. It provides a strong foundation for overcoming adversity and conflict.

Compare Isaiah and Hosea with the commonly accepted notion that justice means each person gets his or her due. For example, honest work and responsible living merit appropriate rewards in terms of standard of living and place in the community. Wrongful behaviors deserve punishment in proportion to how bad they were as defined by social codes, rules, or laws. In either case, justice means a person ought to receive what is due based on the kind or amount of good or bad he or she has done.

In other words, conversations about justice today typically emphasize the following:

Enforcement of laws

The role of the state or civil officials

Unbiased and impartial judges

Individual actions, and what is due and proportionate in response to them (i.e., fairness and equity of response in terms of what individual actions deserve or merit)

A backward-looking perspective to settle accounts from past wrong. According to the Basic Principles, a "restorative outcome" is an agreement reached as a result of a restorative process. The agreement may include referrals to programs such as reparation, restitution and community services, "aimed at meeting the individual and collective needs and responsibilities of the parties and achieving the reintegration of the victim and the offender". It may also be combined with other measures in cases involving serious offences.

As important as those are, Biblical passages such as Isaiah 32, Hosea 2, and others, provide a much larger vision of justice. That vision focuses on people, on individual and social well-being – specifically, on people in right relationship with God and with each other. Biblical justice is fundamentally personal and relational. Moreover, it envisions a full- ness of life for all.

Thus, Biblical justice emphasizes the following:

People and relationships

The well-being of people and relationships

Repair of harm to people and relationships

A forward-looking perspective to restore people and relationships in both present and future states

The Biblical conception of justice is rooted in and stems from the vision of shalom. The Hebrew word for peace, shalom (שלום) is derived from a root denoting wholeness or completeness, and its frame of reference throughout Jewish literature is bound up with the notion of shelemut, perfection.

Its significance is thus not limited to the political domain to the absence of war and enmity or to the social to the absence of quarrel and strife. It ranges over several spheres and can refer in different contexts to bounteous physical conditions, to a moral value, and, ultimately, to a cosmic principle and divine attribute.

Shalom in the Bible is a richly textured idea. Generally translated as peace, shalom means more than a lack of conflict. It envisions people in active, right, fruitful relationships with each other, with God and with creation. Peace in this sense not only reducesor prevents conflict but it also fosters individual and social well-being.It yields a fullness of life for all.

Justice then, biblically understood, seeks shalom. When wrongdoing occurs between people, shalom suffers and it is unjust to leave unresolved both the wrongdoing and the resulting harm. Practicing justice rebuilds and increases shalom for the affected individuals and society.

Accordingly, restorative justice is an attempt to respond to wrong- doers and to the harm they have caused so that relationships within the community are strengthened, injuries are resolved, community values are upheld, and victims are protected.

Biblical dual views of Restorative and Retributive Justice:

What does the Bible say should be the result if a master strikes the eye of a servant and because of it, he/she goes blind? (Exodus 21:26-27):

He shall let him go free for his eye's sake.

Note that the principle of eye for an eye has a different application for servants. The servant, if injured by the master, received something more precious than an eye - his freedom.

However, in Matthew 5:38-39, Jesus recommended: But I say unto you, that ye resist not evil: but whosoever shall smite thee on thy right cheek, turn to him the other also.

When a person insults us (slaps you on the right cheek) our first reaction is to want to give them back what they gave to us, PLUS more. Jesus said we should patiently bear such insults and offences, and not resist an evil person who insults us this way. Instead, we should trust God to defend us.

In contrast, Retributive Justice as we see in common laws and Courts, before pronouncing sentence, the judge enumerated the usual goals of sentences:

a): the need for retribution, b): the need to isolate offenders from society, c): the need to rehabilitate, d): the need to deter.

As we will learn in this book, the judge did not include the goal of restoration. Restoration is a sentencing goal that seeks to address this damage done by making the victim, the community, and even the offender whole again.

Spending time in prison or jail always has profound effects on a young person's future. Many youths, once in the prison system, will stay there for significant portions of their lives. About one-third of all people incarcerated when young return to jail or prison within a few years after release. In addition, if they do manage to stay out of prison, youth who have been incarcerated experience diminished income in comparison with their non-incarcerated peers.

In many cases, most judges as they pronounced their sentence say words similar to this: The Judge admonished the offender, "I trust that there you will forget the patterns of behavior which led to this violent offense. Is this typically the result when a youth is thrust into the prison system for years on end?

Those entering prison while still children must cope with solitary confinement, increased risk of suicide, denied adequate mental health care, and the ever-present sexual, verbal, and physical abuse. Some spend years only fleeting human contact, rather than learning to interact with others properly.

Though these offenders are incarcerated, but the time in prison is not changing them, because they miss what the Defendant attorney suggested which in many occasions changes these individuals.

Instead of this being a confrontation between two individuals regarding restitution, the legal process and the media highlighted the actions of the criminal and only secondarily remembered the victim which is all too often the case in today's legal system.
Finally:

Restorative justice, as practiced in many communities in the world, is a conflict resolution paradigm that brings together the victims, offenders, and community members to address and resolve a crime or a dispute. It aims at restoration, reparation, reintegration, and community participation in tackling crime, disputes, and related problems that affect them.

Restoration takes many forms, such as compensation, reparation or apology, and helps mend broken relationships. In Africa and Asia, this makes perfect sense because peoples tend to live communally and abhorred anything that could strain relationships, disconnect an individual or family with the community, and paralyze their social relationships.

CHAPTER 02

THE TEACHINGS OF JESUS ON JUSTICE

The teachings of Jesus on justice are deeply embedded in the New Testament of the Bible, primarily in the Gospels. Here are some key Bible references that highlight Jesus' teachings on justice:

1. The Sermon on the Mount (Matthew 5-7):

- Matthew 5:6: "Blessed are those who hunger and thirst for righteousness, for they will be filled."

- Matthew 5:9: "Blessed are the peacemakers, for they will be called children of God."

2. The Parable of the Good Samaritan (Luke 10:25-37):

- This parable illustrates the concept of loving your neighbor and shows that true justice involves compassion and action.

3. The Beatitudes (Matthew 5:3-12):

- These teachings emphasize qualities such as meekness, mercy, and purity of heart, which are integral to understanding a just and righteous life.

4. The Golden Rule (Matthew 7:12):

- "So in everything, do to others what you would have them do to you, for this sums up the Law and the Prophets."

5. The Judgment of the Nations (Matthew 25:31-46):

- This passage highlights the importance of caring for the marginalized and disadvantaged as a measure of one's righteousness.

6. Forgiveness and Reconciliation (Matthew 6:14-15; Matthew 18:21-22):

- Jesus' teachings on forgiveness emphasize the importance of reconciliation and mercy.

7. The Rich Young Ruler (Mark 10:17-27):

- This story demonstrates the call to justice and equity, encouraging us to share our wealth and resources with those in need.

These Bible references are just a starting point for understanding Jesus' teachings on justice. His messages consistently emphasize love, compassion, and a commitment to the well-being of others, which are central themes in the concept of restorative justice and its application in various aspects of life.

Mark records Jesus' initial two miracles, both unfolding on the Sabbath: the expulsion of an unclean spirit and the healing of Simon's mother-in-law. Following these impactful acts of compassion, news of Jesus' miracles quickly spreads, with many more unfolding after the Sabbath concludes.

In these inaugural public demonstrations, Jesus exemplifies a profound love and compassion that transcends societal norms. His actions extend to individuals irrespective of their social standing, including the mentally ill, and challenge gender norms by healing a woman. Jesus exhibits unwavering compassion and refuses to be constrained by conventional expectations, even when it comes to the sanctity of the Sabbath. He disregards societal taboos surrounding interactions with the mentally ill or physical contact with a woman, prioritizing a higher calling—the pursuit of healing justice.

This commitment to reaching out to the disenfranchised and marginalized becomes a foundational theme woven throughout the subsequent chapters of Mark's Gospel. Importantly, these acts of compassion are not isolated incidents but rather integral components of a broader narrative. Despite the miraculous nature of these events, their significance lies not in the miracles themselves but in the overarching purpose Jesus articulates: "Let us go on to the nearby villages that I may preach there also. For this purpose, have

I come." In these words, Jesus unveils a profound mission centered on preaching and teaching—a mission that transcends the immediate impact of individual miracles and underscores the transformative power of love and compassion.

The Teachings on Forgiveness and Reconciliation

Another poignant lesson on forgiveness emerges in the wake of a miraculous event, underscoring the inseparable connection between compassion and love. Returning to Capernaum, Jesus finds himself in a packed house, engaged in preaching. In a remarkable display of determination and faith, four individuals lower a paralyzed man through the roof. The nature of the relationship between the four men and the paralyzed individual remains unspecified, but it is reasonable to infer a bond of friendship or familial ties. What becomes evident, however, is the profound faith demonstrated by all four. Unspoken yet palpable in the narrative is the remarkable love and compassion exhibited by these individuals, going to extraordinary lengths to bring the paralyzed man to Jesus for healing. This episode not only imparts a lesson on forgiveness but also serves as a poignant preparation for what unfolds next.

Jesus then boldly declares to the paralyzed man, "Child, your sins are forgiven," a statement that sparks controversy.

When confronted and accused of blasphemy, Jesus responds with a thought-provoking question, "Which is easier, to say to the paralytic, 'Your sins are forgiven,' or to say, 'Rise, pick up your mat and walk?'" This question underscores a profound proposition: forgiveness must precede healing (reconciliation).

The Lessons of Justice:

Within the miracles performed by Jesus, each encapsulating valuable teachings in the Gospel of St. Mark, a consistent underlying message emerges. As previously highlighted, it is Jesus setting aside societal conventions, traditions, and taboos in favor of justice. Illustrated through his acts of healing towards the mentally ill and impoverished, his willingness to touch the infirmed, women, and children, and his healing on the Sabbath, Jesus reinforces the idea that justice is the greater good. Furthermore, he asserts that any obstruction to justice, regardless of its source, has no rightful place ("The Sabbath was made for man, not man for the Sabbath"). The lessons of love and compassion, forgiveness and reconciliation, and justice manifest as intertwined themes throughout the parables and teachings of Jesus Christ in St. Mark's Gospel.

Now, as people following the ways of Jesus Christ, how do we engage in a contemporary context where institutionalized justice often dehumanizes both victim and offender, failing to foster reconciliation on any level? One approach is through Restorative Justice.

The concept revolves around bringing the marginalized and dehumanized to a juncture where order, chaos, limitation, and possibility converge and can commence interaction. However, this is Jesus, the Son of God, transcending the limitations of a mere human being. The question arises: How can an individual or a small group initiate the restoration process, particularly within deeply ingrained societal institutions like the justice industry, fixated on process, punishment, and vengeance, often neglecting the human beings it serves? This seems an almost insurmountable task, especially without resorting to revolutionary measures. Jesus acknowledges this challenge.

In Chapter Four of Mark, Jesus imparts four parables intended to inspire his disciples and anyone with receptive ears. These are the parables of the sower, the lamp, the growing seed, and the mustard seed—or the parables of an open mind, of deeds, and of patient growth. The first parable commences with the imperative "Hear this!"—a call for an active response to what is heard, a command to be obeyed.

The parable of the sower unfolds as Jesus addresses his disciples and the crowd on the shore. It narrates the story of a man sowing seeds, some falling on different types of soil with varying outcomes. Seeds on the path are devoured by birds, those on rocky soil sprout but wither due to insufficient nourishment, and seeds among thorns are strangled. Only those on fertile soil thrive and yield abundant harvests.

One interpretation suggests that the restoration and societal reordering Jesus advocates necessitate an open and fertile mind—a willingness to accept others and engage in love and compassion. The foundational requirement is a seed, representing Jesus' message of love and compassion. Mere dissemination of the message is insufficient; the mind must be open, akin to fertile ground ready to act and produce. Otherwise, as Jesus warns, individuals may see and hear but not understand or be converted and forgiven.

In the parable of the lamp, Jesus raises the question, "Is a lamp brought in to be placed under a bushel basket or under a bed, and not to be placed on a lampstand?" The obvious answer is no, as the lamp's purpose is to provide illumination. This parable becomes a call to action—a reminder that teaching love and compassion is insufficient; one must act upon these lessons. Stand out with the message, let your actions shine like a lamp in the darkness, not hidden away as a secret for only those who know where to look. In doing so, the subsequent aspect of Jesus' message, forgiveness, and reconciliation, can be actualized.

The challenge appears formidable: How does one bring about a comprehensive societal transformation, shifting from a mindset of retribution and punishment to one rooted in forgiveness and reconciliation? The question of feasibility looms large. Once again, Jesus provides insight, affirming that it is indeed possible. Through the parables of the seed's growth (4:26-32), Jesus illustrates that when planted under suitable conditions, even the tiniest seed can autonomously grow into the most substantial of plants. Implicit in this metaphor is the understanding that growth is not instantaneous; it requires time, favorable conditions, and concerted effort. Often, the intricacies of this process evade human comprehension—it simply unfolds.

While these parables explicitly address the growth of the Kingdom of Heaven on earth, they also acknowledge the role of humanity in carrying forth the message. St. Mark has conveyed Jesus' call to action, and now he imparts a message of encouragement and hope—a sort of Biblical "pep talk." The lessons of love, compassion, forgiveness, and reconciliation demand action, yet the realization of this action's impact is a gradual process, requiring sustained effort. The growth of the tiny seed occurs incrementally, eventually giving rise to branches that provide shelter for the birds of the sky (4:32). Similarly, the work of Restorative Justice has the potential to effect a societal reordering and foster a cultural shift, albeit gradually and methodically.

A Cautionary Tale: The Fig Tree's Curse

Following his entry into Jerusalem, Jesus encounters a fig tree outside Bethany covered in leaves but devoid of fruit, as it wasn't the season for figs (11:12-13). Seemingly perplexing to the disciples, Jesus sternly curses the fig tree with the words, "May no one ever eat of your fruit again!" (11:14). The next day, as they pass by, the disciples witness the tree "withered to its roots" (11:20). In response to Peter's comment on the tree's condition, Jesus imparts a profound message:

"Have faith in God. Amen I say to you, whoever says to this mountain, 'Be lifted up and thrown into the sea.' And does not doubt in his heart but believes that what he says will happen; it shall be done for him. Therefore, I tell you, all that you ask for in prayer, believe that you will receive it and it shall be yours. When you stand to pray, forgive anyone against whom you have a grievance, so your heavenly Father may in turn forgive you your transgressions" (11:22-25).

Contextualized between these passages is Jesus' entry into the temple in Jerusalem and his subsequent expulsion of money changers and sellers (11:15-17). Viewed in this context, the curse on the fig tree and its subsequent withering serve as a condemnation of the temple of Israel.

In the Septuagint and the New Testament, "time" is referenced as an opportune moment. The temple, akin to the fig tree full of leaves but barren of fruit, symbolizes an institution that outwardly satisfies the needs of the people. However, it fails to fulfill its purpose, perpetually waiting for an opportune moment. As the hub of Judaic culture, regulating religious, political, economic, and social life, the temple becomes the target of Jesus' disapproval. Withholding access to God for an opportune moment is deemed unacceptable by Jesus. Just as he curses the unproductive fig tree, he condemns the temple institution.

Hence, the curse of the fig tree serves not only as an emphatic punctuation mark to Jesus' previous teachings but also as a warning to those who might undermine his message or become complacent in an institution that caters only to those in control. It signals an opportune time for social justice through forgiveness and reconciliation—one that should not be overlooked or ignored.

CONCLUSION

The teachings of Jesus Christ, as preserved in the Gospel of St. Mark, offer a direct connection to the earliest synoptic gospels—

a profound source that echoes the foundation of a new social order centered on justice. Jesus' message and lessons on justice are anchored in love, compassion, forgiveness, and reconciliation, distinctly diverging from obstructive procedures and vengeance-driven retribution. This message serves as a compelling call to action, urging a commitment to tangible work over mere rhetoric.

One potent manifestation of such action is found in Restorative Justice—a versatile approach shaped by cultural nuances rather than rigid processes. By actively seeking reconciliation between victims and offenders, Restorative Justice inherently involves the affected community. Addressing the needs, obligations, and responsibilities of victims, offenders, and the community at large, this approach catalyzes a reordering of the social fabric. Consequently, justice transforms into an interpersonal and community-based endeavor, departing from institutional norms that often treat individuals and communities as mere components of a procedural system rather than its central focus.

Recognizing the apparent enormity of the task at hand, Jesus offers a poignant reminder that the pursuit of justice and peace is an enduring journey requiring time and effort. Analogous to the tiny mustard seed falling on fertile ground and nurtured by the sower, this endeavor has the transformative potential to blossom into one of the greatest trees. The call for a shift in attitude and character is not a distant prospect—it is an imperative for the present moment. The time for embracing this profound change is now.

CHAPTER 03

PARABLES AND RESTORATIVE JUSTICE

Parables are powerful stories told by Jesus in the New Testament of the Bible. They often contain moral or spiritual lessons and can be related to the concept of restorative justice in several ways:

1. The Prodigal Son (Luke 15:11-32): This parable is a profound illustration of forgiveness and restoration. The father's response to the wayward son, who repents and returns home, exemplifies the restorative approach. Instead of punitive measures, the father forgives and restores his son, emphasizing the transformative power of mercy.

2. The Unforgiving Servant (Matthew 18:21-35): In this parable, Jesus highlights the importance of forgiveness in the context of restorative justice. The unforgiving servant is forgiven a great debt but refuses to show the same mercy to someone who owes him. The message is clear: those who have received mercy should extend it to others, promoting reconciliation.

3. The Good Samaritan (Luke 10:25-37): The parable of the Good Samaritan underlines the concept of compassion and care for others, especially those who are marginalized or in need. It serves as a call to action, emphasizing the restorative principles of helping and healing the wounded.

4. The Lost Sheep and the Lost Coin (Luke 15:3-10): These parables emphasize the importance of seeking out and restoring what is lost. They illustrate the idea that everyone has intrinsic value and should be actively pursued for reconciliation and restoration.

5. The Workers in the Vineyard (Matthew 20:1-16): This parable challenges notions of fairness and reward. It illustrates the idea that everyone, regardless of when they come to faith or seek redemption, can receive God's grace. It reflects the restorative concept of offering opportunities for change and reintegration.

These parables, among others, provide powerful narratives that align with restorative justice principles. They emphasize themes of forgiveness, reconciliation, compassion, and the restoration of relationships. These parables can serve as a source of inspiration for understanding how restorative justice can be applied in various aspects of life, from criminal justice to community building and personal relationships.

CHAPTER 04

FORGIVENESS AND RECONCILIATION

Forgiveness and reconciliation are central themes in both the teachings of Jesus and the concept of restorative justice. Here's an overview of how these concepts are interwoven:

Forgiveness:

1. Teachings of Jesus: Jesus emphasized forgiveness in many of his teachings. In the Lord's Prayer (Matthew 6:9-13), he instructs his followers to pray, "Forgive us our debts, as we also have forgiven our debtors." This underscores the idea that forgiveness is a reciprocal action.

2. Parables: Parables like the Unforgiving Servant (Matthew 18:21-35) convey the importance of forgiving others. In this parable, a servant who is forgiven a large debt refuses to extend the same forgiveness to a fellow servant, resulting in consequences. The message is clear: forgiveness is essential.

3. Restorative Justice: Restorative justice embraces the idea that forgiveness is a key component of the healing process. It allows victims and offenders to come to terms with the harm that was done and, in some cases, facilitates the exchange of apologies and amends.

Reconciliation:

1. Teachings of Jesus: Jesus' message of reconciliation is epitomized in passages such as the Sermon on the Mount, where he encourages peacemaking (Matthew 5:9). Reconciliation implies not only the absence of conflict but also the restoration of relationships.

2. The Prodigal Son Parable: In the Parable of the Prodigal Son (Luke 15:11-32), the father's open arms symbolize reconciliation. He doesn't just welcome back his wayward son; he restores him to his rightful place in the family.

3. Restorative Justice: Restorative justice is fundamentally about restoring relationships and reintegrating offenders into their communities. It provides a structured framework for victims and offenders to come together, address the harm, and work towards reconciliation.

Both forgiveness and reconciliation are pivotal in the application of restorative justice. They emphasize the transformation of conflict and harm into opportunities for healing and growth, aligning with the compassionate and merciful teachings of Jesus. These principles have practical applications in criminal justice, community disputes, and personal relationships, as they promote understanding, repair, and the rebuilding of trust.

CHAPTER 05

RESTORATIVE JUSTICE IN BIBLICAL CONTEXT AND IN THE CHURCH

Biblical Restorative Justice is a framework for justice that is grounded in the teachings of the Bible, and emphasizes the importance of repairing harm caused by wrongdoing, reconciling relationships, and restoring wholeness to individuals and communities. It is based on the idea that justice is not just about punishing offenders, but also about healing and restoring both victims and offenders.

Restorative justice seeks to address the root causes of conflict and harm, and to bring about a transformation in the lives of both the victim and the offender. It is based on the belief that all individuals are created in the image of God and have inherent dignity and worth, and that justice should be focused on restoring that dignity and worth.

Restorative justice is practiced through processes such as victim-offender mediation, community conferencing, and family group conferencing, which bring together those affected by a crime or conflict to talk about the harm that has been done and to find ways to repair that harm. This approach seeks to promote healing, forgiveness, and reconciliation, and to create a sense of community ownership and responsibility for justice.

Biblical Restorative Justice is based on a number of key principles, including:

1. The importance of community: Restorative justice is grounded in the belief that individuals are interconnected and that communities have an important role to play in promoting justice and healing.
2. The value of relationships: Restorative justice emphasizes the importance of repairing relationships that have been damaged by wrongdoing, and seeks to create opportunities for dialogue and understanding between victims and offenders.
3. The need for accountability: Restorative justice recognizes the importance of holding offenders accountable for their actions, while also providing them with opportunities to take responsibility for repairing the harm they have caused.
4. The importance of healing and restoration: Restorative justice focuses on restoring wholeness to individuals and communities that have been impacted by crime or conflict, and seeks to promote healing, forgiveness, and reconciliation.

Thus, Biblical Restorative Justice is an approach to justice that seeks to promote healing, reconciliation, and restoration and is grounded in the belief that all individuals are created in the image of God and have inherent dignity and worth.

Biblical restorative justice implementation:

Implementing Biblical restorative justice requires a commitment to the principles and values of this approach to justice, and a willingness to engage in a process that seeks to repair harm, reconcile relationships, and restore wholeness to individuals and communities. Here are some steps that can be taken to implement Biblical restorative justice:

1. Education and Training: Educate yourself and others about the principles and values of Biblical restorative justice. This may involve attending training sessions, workshops, and seminars to learn about the concepts and processes involved in this approach.

2. Engagement with the Community: Engage with the community to build relationships and promote a sense of shared responsibility for justice. This can involve reaching out to local organizations, churches, and community leaders to promote awareness of restorative justice principles and values.

3. Development of Restorative Justice Processes: Develop restorative justice processes that are appropriate for your community and the specific circumstances of each case. This may involve implementing victim-offender mediation programs, community conferencing, or other forms of restorative justice that promote dialogue and understanding between victims and offenders.

4. Establishment of Support Systems: Establish support systems for both victims and offenders. This may involve providing counseling, mentorship, or other forms of support to help individuals process the harm that has been done and to promote healing and restoration.

5. Integration with the Justice System: Integrate restorative justice principles and practices with the broader justice system. This may involve collaborating with law enforcement, courts, and other justice system stakeholders to promote the use of restorative justice in appropriate cases.

6. Evaluation and Improvement: Evaluate the effectiveness of restorative justice processes and make improvements as needed. This may involve monitoring outcomes such as victim satisfaction, offender recidivism rates, and community relations, and making adjustments to the restorative justice approach as needed.

Accordingly, implementing Biblical restorative justice requires a commitment to building relationships, promoting healing, and restoring wholeness to individuals and communities. This approach to justice requires a shift in mindset and a willingness to prioritize repairing harm over punishment and retribution.

In the church context, restorative justice involves:

1. Biblical Foundation: Restorative justice in the church is firmly grounded in the Bible, especially in the teachings of the Apostle Paul in the Book of Romans. It draws from these theological underpinnings to shape the church's approach to addressing harm and conflict.

2. Congregational Engagement: The church community actively engages with restorative justice principles. This encompasses not only understanding and discussing these principles but putting them into practice within the church's internal affairs.

3. Conflict Resolution: Restorative justice in the church provides a framework for resolving conflicts, promoting healing, and maintaining unity among church members. It encourages open communication, understanding, and reconciliation.

4. Ministry and Outreach: The church extends its involvement in restorative justice beyond its own walls. It plays a role in addressing broader societal issues, such as supporting those affected by crime, advocating for criminal justice reform, and promoting healing and reconciliation in the community.

5. Victim Support: The church offers support and care for victims, acknowledging their suffering, and helping them on their journey to healing. It prioritizes the restoration of dignity for those who have been harmed.

6. Promoting Reconciliation: Restorative justice in the church places a strong emphasis on the power of reconciliation, both within the church community and in the wider world. It encourages the restoration of broken relationships and the building of bridges between individuals and communities.

7. Moral Leadership: The church serves as a moral leader, advocating for restorative justice principles in the criminal justice system. It speaks out against punitive measures and promotes a vision of justice that emphasizes rehabilitation, reconciliation, and healing.

In essence, restorative justice in the church reflects the application of Christian values and theological principles to address harm, resolve conflicts, and promote healing and reconciliation. It recognizes the church as a powerful force for transformation and justice within the Christian community and the broader society.

The biblical foundation of restorative justice in the Book of Romans is deeply rooted in the teachings of the Apostle Paul and the theological principles he expounds in this epistle. These teachings provide a strong biblical basis for restorative justice principles. Here's how the Book of Romans forms the foundation:

1. Reconciliation: The central theme of reconciliation runs throughout the Book of Romans. In Romans 5:10 (NIV), Paul writes, "For if, while we were God's enemies, we were reconciled to him through the death of his Son, how much more, having been reconciled, shall we be saved through his life!" This verse underscores the idea of reconciliation, which is fundamental in restorative justice. It emphasizes the restoration of relationships and the healing of divisions.

2. Forgiveness: Romans also addresses the concept of forgiveness. In Romans 12:19-21 (NIV), Paul exhorts, "Do not take revenge, my dear friends, but leave room for God's wrath, for it is written: 'It is mine to avenge; I will repay,' says the Lord. On the contrary: 'If your enemy is hungry, feed him; if he is thirsty, give him something to drink. In doing this, you will hear burning coals on his head.'" This passage highlights the Christian value of forgiveness, a core principle in restorative justice.

3. Love and Compassion: Love and compassion are central to restorative justice. Romans 13:10 (NIV) states, "Love does no

harm to a neighbor. Therefore, love is the fulfillment of the law." This verse emphasizes the importance of love and non-harm, which are foundational principles in restorative justice practices.

4. Accountability: Romans teaches the concept of accountability. In Romans 14:12 (NIV), it says, "So then, each of us will give an account of ourselves to God." This verse highlights personal accountability, a crucial element in the restorative justice process.

5. Transformation: Romans speaks of personal transformation and renewal through faith in Christ. Romans 12:2 (NIV) states, "Do not conform to the pattern of this world but be transformed by the renewing of your mind." Transformation is a key aspect of restorative justice, as it signifies a commitment to change one's behavior and contribute positively to society.

6. Justice and Mercy: The Book of Romans grapples with the balance between justice and mercy, reflecting the tension often present in restorative justice practices. Romans 9:15 (NIV) addresses the concept of God's mercy, "I will have mercy on whom I have mercy, and I will have compassion on whom I have compassion." Restorative justice seeks to harmonize justice and mercy, just as the Book of Romans does.

The Book of Romans, with its emphasis on reconciliation, forgiveness, love, accountability, transformation, and the interplay of justice and mercy, provides a robust biblical foundation for restorative justice principles. These teachings align with core Christian values and offer guidance on how individuals and communities can address harm, promote healing, and restore relationships by their faith.

Congregational engagement in the practices of restorative justice within the Christian church can have a profoundly positive impact. Here are several ways in which this engagement can influence and enhance restorative justice practices:

1. Promoting Understanding: Congregational engagement involves educating and involving the church community in understanding the principles of restorative justice. This can include sermons, study groups, and workshops that help members grasp the theological and practical aspects of restorative justice. A well-informed congregation is better equipped to support and implement these principles.

2. Creating a Supportive Environment: The church community can become a safe and supportive environment for those affected by harm or conflict. Congregational members can offer emotional and spiritual support to victims and offenders, recognizing the importance of healing and reconciliation.

3. Conflict Resolution: The church can actively use restorative justice principles to address conflicts and disagreements within the congregation. This approach fosters open dialogue, understanding, and reconciliation, preventing issues from escalating and creating division.

4. Accountability: The church can model accountability by holding individuals responsible for their actions. This is vital in demonstrating the principles of restorative justice, as it emphasizes personal responsibility and the consequences of one's behavior.

5. Reconciliation: The congregation can actively promote reconciliation and restoration of relationships, not only within the church but also in the broader community. The church can serve as a beacon of hope, showing that forgiveness, healing, and unity are possible.

6. Ministry and Outreach: Engaging in restorative justice practices means extending support to those beyond the church community. This may involve advocating for criminal justice reform, supporting victims of crime, and offering healing and reconciliation to the broader society.

7. Moral Leadership: The church, through its leaders and members, can provide moral leadership in advocating for restorative justice principles in the broader society. It can be a strong voice for alternatives to punitive justice systems, emphasizing rehabilitation and reconciliation.

8. Victim Support: The congregation can actively engage in supporting victims, acknowledging their suffering, and helping them on their journey to healing. This support is essential in restoring the dignity of those who have been harmed.

9. Teaching and Modeling Love and Forgiveness: The church community can teach and model Christian values of love and forgiveness, which are core principles of restorative justice. Congregational members can exemplify these values in their interactions with one another and the broader community.

10. Promoting Transformation: Encouraging personal transformation is a vital part of restorative justice. The congregation can provide an environment that supports individuals in their commitment to change, contributing positively to society.

Congregational engagement positively affects the practices of restorative justice by creating a well-informed, supportive, and accountable community that actively promotes understanding, reconciliation, and the application of Christian values. The church can serve as a living example of the restorative justice principles found in the teachings of the Apostle Paul in the Book of Romans, inspiring individuals to seek healing, forgiveness, and reconciliation.

Conflict resolution within the church is a vital aspect of maintaining unity and harmony among its members. Restorative justice principles, inspired by the teachings of Romans, can offer effective tools for addressing conflicts and promoting healing within the church community. Here's how conflict resolution can align with these principles:

1. Open Dialogue: Restorative justice encourages open and honest dialogue. In conflicts within the church, this means providing a safe space for those involved to express their concerns, perspectives, and emotions. Encouraging open communication is in line with the principle of addressing harm and understanding one another.

2. Understanding the Impact: Restorative justice asks individuals to consider the impact of their actions on others. In conflict resolution, this means helping parties involved in the dispute to understand how their words or actions have affected others. It fosters empathy and compassion, which are essential for healing and reconciliation.

3. Accountability: Restorative justice emphasizes personal responsibility. In the context of church conflict resolution, this means encouraging those involved to take responsibility for their words or actions that contributed to the dispute. Acknowledging one's role in the conflict is a crucial step in the restoration process.

4. Making Amends: Just as making amends is central to restorative justice, it's essential in resolving church conflicts. Parties involved can work together to find ways to repair the harm caused.

This may involve apologies, acts of service, or other gestures of reconciliation.

5. Reconciliation: Restorative justice seeks reconciliation as its ultimate goal. In church conflict resolution, the focus should be on rebuilding relationships and promoting unity. Encouraging forgiveness and seeking reconciliation align with the principles found in the Book of Romans.

6. Community Involvement: Restorative justice often involves the wider community in the resolution process. In the context of church conflicts, this can mean seeking advice or mediation from church leaders, elders, or congregation members who can support the resolution efforts.

7. Restoring Dignity: The church should always seek to restore the dignity of those involved in the conflict. Treating each party with respect and acknowledging their worth as individuals created in God's image is essential for the healing process.

8. Transformation and Renewal: Restorative justice encourages personal transformation. In the church, this transformation may involve a change in behavior, attitudes, or perspectives, allowing individuals to contribute positively to the community and prevent future conflicts.

9. Forgiveness and Repentance: Encouraging forgiveness and repentance is integral to resolving conflicts in the church. Embracing these principles aligns with the Christian values of love, grace, and reconciliation found in Romans.

By applying these restorative justice principles, church leaders and members can effectively resolve conflicts, promote healing, and maintain unity within the church community. These principles offer a pathway to address disputes in a way that reflects the teachings of the Apostle Paul in Romans, fostering a culture of understanding, forgiveness, and reconciliation.

Ministry and outreach in the context of the Book of Romans and restorative justice encompass a broad and impactful approach to addressing societal issues. Here are some ways in which churches can engage in ministry and outreach inspired by restorative justice principles:

1. Supporting Victims: Churches can provide vital support for individuals who have been victims of crime. This can include

counseling, emotional support, and practical assistance. Restorative justice encourages empathy and care for those who have suffered harm, aligning with the Christian values of compassion and love.

2. Advocating for Criminal Justice Reform: Restorative justice principles emphasize a shift from punitive to restorative measures. Churches can engage in advocacy efforts for criminal justice reform, pushing for policies that emphasize rehabilitation, reintegration, and addressing the root causes of crime.

3. Reentry Programs: Supporting individuals reintegrating into society after serving time in the criminal justice system is crucial. Churches can establish reentry programs that provide resources, mentorship, and a supportive community for those looking to rebuild their lives. This aligns with restorative justice's emphasis on transformation and renewal.

4. Community Building: Restorative justice is about repairing harm and building stronger, more harmonious communities. Churches can engage in community-building initiatives, fostering relationships, trust, and unity among their members and the broader community.

5. Restorative Practices: Churches can incorporate restorative practices within their own community, using restorative circles or mediation to address conflicts and promote healing. These practices can be extended to the community at large, helping resolve disputes and foster reconciliation.

6. Restorative Justice Education: Educating the congregation and the community about restorative justice principles, their biblical foundations, and their practical applications can empower individuals to engage in these practices in their own lives and support them in wider society.

7. Social Justice Initiatives: Addressing societal injustices is a fundamental aspect of restorative justice. Churches can initiate and support social justice campaigns that tackle issues such as poverty, inequality, racism, and discrimination. These efforts align with the principles of addressing harm and promoting equity.

8. Prison Ministry: Engaging in prison ministry provides spiritual and emotional support to incarcerated individuals. It can also be a platform for sharing restorative justice principles, offering hope for personal transformation and redemption.

9. Victim-Offender Dialogue: Encouraging victim-offender dialogue and reconciliation processes can be part of the outreach efforts. These dialogues can help both victims and offenders find closure and healing, in line with restorative justice goals.

10. Refugee and Migrant Support: Churches can actively support refugees and migrants, helping them find shelter, resources, and community. Restorative justice principles emphasize empathy and hospitality, which align with the support needed by those forced to leave their homes.

In summary, ministry and outreach in the context of the Book of Romans and restorative justice entail a comprehensive and compassionate approach to addressing societal issues. It involves supporting victims, advocating for reform, providing reentry programs, building community, practicing restorative approaches, and actively engaging with social justice initiatives. Through these actions, churches can extend the principles of restorative justice to create a more just, compassionate, and reconciled society.

Victim support is imperative for several significant reasons, and the church plays a vital role in this crucial aspect of restorative justice:

1. Compassion and Empathy: One of the core principles of restorative justice is empathy and compassion for those who have suffered harm. The church, rooted in Christian teachings, exemplifies these values by extending care and support to victims. This not only aligns with Christian values but also with the restorative justice goal of acknowledging the pain of victims.

2. Healing and Restoration: Victims often go through a traumatic experience that can leave lasting emotional and psychological scars. The church can provide a safe space for victims to heal, seek counseling, and find comfort in their faith. This healing process is essential for restoring victims' well-being, in line with restorative justice's focus on repairing harm.

3. Dignity and Worth: Restorative justice places a strong emphasis on recognizing the inherent dignity and worth of every individual. Supporting victims in their journey to recovery and justice restoration is a practical way to affirm their dignity. The church's role in this process aligns with the Christian belief in the sanctity of human life.

4. Rebuilding Trust: Victims may often feel a loss of trust in their community and the world at large. The church, through its support, can contribute to rebuilding trust in others, as well as trust in the possibility of healing and restoration. This restoration of trust is a fundamental aspect of restorative justice.

5. Community and Belonging: The church serves as a community of faith and belonging. By providing support for victims, it reinforces the idea that victims are not alone in their suffering. Restorative justice seeks to repair the social bonds that are strained by harm, and the church plays a key role in reestablishing a sense of community.

6. Moral and Ethical Responsibility: For the church, extending support to victims is a moral and ethical responsibility. It reflects the Christian commitment to love, compassion, and helping those in need. This sense of responsibility resonates with the restorative justice principle of addressing the needs of those who have been harmed.

7. Promoting Forgiveness and Reconciliation: Restorative justice encourages processes of forgiveness and reconciliation. While these are personal journeys, the church can offer guidance and a spiritual foundation for individuals seeking to forgive or reconcile with those who have caused harm.

8. Advocacy for Victims: The church can also play a role in advocating for the rights and needs of victims within the wider community and even in the criminal justice system. This advocacy is in alignment with the restorative justice principle of ensuring that victims have a voice in the process.

In conclusion, victim support is imperative for its role in healing, restoring dignity, and rebuilding trust for those who have experienced harm. The church, driven by its Christian values, has a unique responsibility in this regard and plays a crucial part in implementing restorative justice principles. By providing support and care to victims, the church contributes to a more compassionate and just society.

Promoting reconciliation within the Christian community involves the active participation of various individuals and groups. Here are key stakeholders involved in fostering reconciliation:

1. Church Leaders: Church leaders, including pastors, priests, and elders, play a pivotal role in promoting reconciliation.

They can provide guidance, counsel, and pastoral care to individuals and families in conflict. Their leadership can set the tone for the entire congregation.

2. Church Members: The congregation itself is a significant part of the reconciliation process. Church members can support one another in times of conflict, offer forgiveness, and extend a helping hand to those in need. The church community is ideally positioned to model reconciliation for the broader society.

3. Counselors and Mediators: Trained counselors and mediators can be valuable resources within the church. They can facilitate communication, help resolve disputes, and guide individuals and families toward reconciliation. Their expertise is especially important when conflicts involve complex dynamics.

4. Families: The church places a strong emphasis on the importance of family. Families are often at the heart of conflicts, and their involvement is essential for reconciliation. Parents, children, and extended family members can work together to heal relational wounds and restore harmony.

5. Small Groups and Support Networks: Many churches organize small groups and support networks. These settings provide opportunities for individuals to share their struggles, receive emotional support, and explore ways to reconcile with one another.

6. Community Engagement: Reconciliation isn't limited to internal church matters. Churches can engage with the broader community to promote reconciliation in society at large. This can involve outreach programs, community service, and advocacy for peace and reconciliation.

7. Prayer and Spiritual Guidance: Prayer and spiritual guidance are central to the Christian approach to reconciliation. The church community can come together in prayer to seek God's guidance and strength in the process of reconciliation.

8. Restorative Justice Ministries: Some churches have specialized ministries or teams dedicated to restorative justice. These groups are focused on addressing conflicts, promoting healing, and actively practicing restorative justice principles within the church and in the community.

9. Youth and Children: Younger members of the church play a significant role in fostering reconciliation. Youth groups and

children's ministries can instill values of forgiveness, empathy, and conflict resolution from an early age, contributing to a culture of reconciliation in the future.

10. Outreach to the Marginalized: The church can engage in outreach to marginalized and vulnerable individuals and communities, offering reconciliation and healing to those who have been excluded or harmed by society.

11. Reconciliation Services: Some churches hold specific reconciliation services or events, where individuals are encouraged to come forward and seek forgiveness or reconciliation with others. These services can be powerful catalysts for healing and unity.

12. Education and Awareness: Churches can educate their members about the importance of reconciliation, forgiveness, and restorative justice. By raising awareness, they empower individuals to actively pursue reconciliation in their lives.

In conclusion, promoting reconciliation within the Christian community involves the collective efforts of church leaders, members, counselors, families, small groups, and the wider community. It's a collaborative endeavor guided by Christian principles of forgiveness, healing, and restoration.

Moral leadership in the context of restorative justice within the church involves the church community and its leaders taking a principled and ethical stand in advocating for restorative practices in the criminal justice system. Here are key aspects of moral leadership in this context:

1. Advocating for Compassion: Moral leaders within the church promote compassion as a central value in the criminal justice system. They emphasize the need to view offenders as individuals in need of healing and restoration, rather than solely as wrongdoers deserving punishment.

2. Rehabilitation Over Retribution: Moral leadership encourages a shift from retribution-focused approaches to rehabilitation-focused ones. Leaders advocate for policies and practices that prioritize the rehabilitation of offenders, aiming to address the root causes of their actions and prevent future harm.

3. Supporting Victim-Centered Approaches: Moral leaders acknowledge the importance of supporting victims of crime and advocating for their needs. They work to ensure that restorative justice practices prioritize the healing and well-being of victims,

allowing them to participate in the process and have their voices heard.

4. Promoting Reconciliation: The church's moral leadership emphasizes the transformative power of reconciliation. Leaders encourage criminal justice systems to incorporate restorative justice principles that facilitate dialogue, forgiveness, and the rebuilding of trust between offenders and victims.

5. Healing and Restoration: Moral leaders advocate for the inclusion of healing and restoration as core components of the criminal justice process. They recognize that true justice involves not only addressing the harm caused by offenses but also helping individuals rebuild their lives in a positive and productive manner.

6. Addressing Systemic Injustices: Church leaders, as moral advocates, address systemic injustices within the criminal justice system. They work to eliminate disparities and biases that disproportionately affect marginalized and vulnerable populations.

7. Educational Initiatives: Moral leaders within the church take an active role in educating their congregations and the broader community about the principles of restorative justice. They raise awareness of the potential for transformation and healing through these practices.

8. Prayer and Spiritual Guidance: Moral leaders engage in prayer and spiritual guidance to seek wisdom and guidance in their advocacy for restorative justice. They encourage their congregations to pray for both victims and offenders, emphasizing the importance of spiritual support in the healing process.

9. Community Engagement: Moral leadership extends beyond the walls of the church. Church leaders engage with the broader community, law enforcement agencies, policymakers, and advocacy groups to promote restorative justice principles and advocate for criminal justice reform.

10. Policy and Legislative Advocacy: Moral leaders may engage in policy and legislative advocacy to bring about changes in the criminal justice system. They work with lawmakers to develop and support legislation that aligns with restorative justice principles.

11. Nonviolent Resistance: Moral leaders may advocate for nonviolent resistance to oppressive or punitive measures within the

criminal justice system. This can include peaceful protests, civil disobedience, and public awareness campaigns.

In summary, moral leadership within the church involves advocating for a compassionate, healing-oriented, and reconciliatory approach to criminal justice. It is rooted in the principles of love, forgiveness, and the pursuit of justice as seen in the teachings of Jesus Christ, as well as in the teachings of Romans on restorative justice.

Case Studies:

Case studies are real-life examples or stories that illustrate the practical application of restorative justice principles within the Christian community. They are essential for several reasons:

1. Concrete Illustration: Case studies provide concrete and tangible examples of how restorative justice is put into practice. They give readers a clear understanding of how the principles discussed in theory are applied in real-life situations.

2. Inspiration: Case studies can inspire individuals, churches, and communities to adopt restorative justice practices. When people see successful examples and positive outcomes, they are more likely to become motivated to implement similar approaches.

3. Learning Opportunities: By examining case studies, readers can learn from both the successes and challenges faced by others. They can gain insights into what works well and what pitfalls to avoid when implementing restorative justice within a Christian context.

4. Contextual Relevance: Case studies can be tailored to specific contexts, allowing readers to relate to situations and challenges that are similar to their own. This contextual relevance makes the application of restorative justice more relatable and achievable.

5. Testimonials of Transformation: Case studies often highlight stories of personal transformation, redemption, and reconciliation. These stories emphasize the positive impact of restorative justice and demonstrate that individuals can change and make amends.

6. Demonstration of Christian Values: Case studies can showcase how restorative justice aligns with Christian values of love, forgiveness, and reconciliation. They demonstrate how the

principles derived from the teachings of Romans can be put into action.

7. Building Support: Sharing successful case studies can help build support for restorative justice initiatives within the church and the broader community. They serve as evidence of the effectiveness of these practices.

8. Challenge Stereotypes: Case studies can challenge stereotypes and preconceptions about offenders and victims. They humanize the individuals involved and show that everyone has the potential for healing and transformation.

9. Promoting Accountability: Case studies often highlight the importance of accountability and making amends, emphasizing that justice can be achieved through actions that repair harm.

10. Fostering Dialogue: These real-life stories can foster dialogue and discussion within the church community, encouraging members to consider the practical application of restorative justice principles in their own lives.

In the context of restorative justice in the church, case studies serve as powerful tools for both education and advocacy. They demonstrate that restorative justice is not just a theoretical concept but a practical and effective approach that can lead to healing, reconciliation, and transformation within the Christian community.

CHAPTER 06

HISTORICAL PERSPECTIVE OF JUSTICE

Historical perspectives on justice have evolved significantly over time, reflecting changes in societies, philosophies, and systems of governance. Here's a brief overview of how justice has been perceived and practiced at different points in history:

1. Ancient Civilizations: In ancient societies, justice often involved retribution and retaliation. The Code of Hammurabi in ancient Babylon is a prime example, with the principle "an eye for an eye" reflecting a form of proportional justice.

2. Classical Antiquity: Greek and Roman philosophers, such as Plato and Aristotle, began to introduce ideas of justice as virtue and fairness. They contemplated concepts of distributive justice, emphasizing the importance of proportionality and equity.

3. Medieval Europe: During the Middle Ages, justice was closely intertwined with religious and feudal systems. The Church played a significant role in defining and administering justice, while feudal lords exercised authority over their territories.

4. Enlightenment Era: The Age of Enlightenment brought about significant changes in how justice was conceptualized. Philosophers like John Locke and Jean-Jacques Rousseau contributed to the idea of justice as a social contract, where citizens voluntarily agreed to a system of laws for the common good.

5. Modern Legal Systems: The development of modern legal systems, including the establishment of democratic institutions and the rule of law, has shaped contemporary perspectives on justice. This era introduced concepts like due process, the presumption of innocence, and the separation of powers.

6. Social Justice Movements: The 20th century saw the emergence of social justice movements, addressing issues of inequality, civil rights, and human rights. These movements expanded the notion of justice to encompass not only legal matters but also social and economic equity.

7. Restorative Justice: More recently, the concept of restorative justice has gained prominence, emphasizing reconciliation, healing, and community involvement as crucial components of justice. This approach contrasts with punitive models and focuses on repairing harm.

Historical perspectives on justice reveal an evolving understanding of the term, moving from punitive measures to more nuanced concepts that consider fairness, equity, and reconciliation. These historical shifts reflect changing societal values, philosophical insights, and the ongoing pursuit of a more just and equitable world.

Hence, Restorative justice is not a novel concept; its roots extend far back in time, finding historical precedence in Africa well before the era of Western European colonization of the continent. Although its efficacy has undergone shifts in the Western criminal justice system, a resurgence of interest is evident (Wyk, 2016). Scholars like Llwelyn and Howse (2002) posit that this revival marks a return to traditional conflict resolution methods worldwide. Numerous studies assert that the origins of restorative justice run deep in Africa and various global regions, regardless of the nomenclature employed (Mangena, 2011).

In Tanzania, for instance, the practice of restorative justice spans millennia. Among the Kinga community in Southern Tanzania, conflicts between family members or clans were traditionally addressed through restorative justice mechanisms. When disputes arose, the involved community convened meetings for reconciliation. Seated in a circular arrangement around a communal fire, resembling a court setting called Lugono, community members engaged in a dialogue. A complainant would recount the incident, and the defendant(s) responded to the accusations, presenting their defense (Ilomo, 2013).

The reconciliation process reached its culmination with a communal sharing of locally brewed alcohol, referred to as 'ukupelanila ulupelo,' and the consumption of roasted meat, known as 'okukatelanila inyama.' The latter involved the disputants cutting a piece of roasted meat, with each party consuming their share. Additionally, a symbolic act of reconciliation occurred through the blowing of a special medicinal substance, termed 'ukupulilanila untuguva,' into each individual's face (Ilomo, 2013). This multifaceted approach to conflict resolution showcases the rich historical tapestry of restorative justice practices in Tanzania, highlighting its cultural significance and enduring legacy.

The approach to resolving conflicts and reconciling involved parties varied based on the severity of the wrongdoing and the number of individuals implicated. Minor conflicts, such as one member insulting another, were typically left to the direct involvement of the parties concerned for resolution. However, more serious offenses or disputes necessitated the engagement of clan members and the broader community. In such instances, community members gathered around a communal fireplace, attentively listening to the conflicting parties. Through questioning and dialogue, they assisted in unraveling the complexities of the problem and uncovering the truth. Notably, the restorative justice system distinguished itself by prioritizing the pursuit of truth, focusing on understanding the root causes of disputes rather than the conventional system's emphasis on convincing others of innocence (Ilomo, 2013).

For the offender in these scenarios, truth-telling was pivotal. They had to voluntarily confess or acknowledge responsibility for their words, actions, or inaction that resulted in harm to the victim and their family. Additionally, displaying genuine remorse for these actions was a prerequisite. Once the truth was revealed, accepted, and responsibility acknowledged, the path to reconciliation unfolded naturally. Repairing and restoring the fractured relationship became the central objective of the restorative justice model. Reconciliation, a cornerstone of this approach, could only occur after all parties—offender, victim, and community members—heard each other's perspectives and established the truth. In situations where a victim endured further harm or suffering due to the perceived wrongdoing or recalcitrance of the community member suspected to be at fault, blame was attributed to the suspect. Consequently, communities recognized the urgency of swiftly resolving conflicts through the restorative justice system to prevent additional harm (Ilomo, 2013).

Similarly, in Nigeria, where various communities have embraced restorative justice practices, Omale (2006) underscores the significance of reconciliation and its ceremonial aspects:

To ensure genuine reconciliation following dispute mediation, both parties may partake in shared activities, such as eating from the same bowl, drinking palm wine, burukutu, or local gin from the same cup, and breaking and consuming kola-nuts.

African communities, guided by their collective wisdom, recognized that the social cohesion of their people rested on truth, understanding the root causes of community issues, and the practice of reconciliation. Unearthing the truth behind events and motives necessitated the active involvement of all community members in candid discussions about specific wrongs, problems, conflicts, or sets of issues. Consequently, African community conflict resolution mechanisms empowered ordinary people to freely participate in addressing disputes and crimes without interference from a centralized and distant state authority. In contrast, post-independence African countries have shifted to state organs handling conflicts and disputes through an adversarial and retributive process, particularly in criminal justice. While these foreign justice processes are not inherently malicious, they are susceptible to significant delays, especially in criminal trials where securing state witnesses proves challenging (Omale, 2006).

Post-independence African nations have predominantly relied on the legal systems introduced by their colonial masters. However, these foreign systems have not proven effective in resolving the multitude of conflicts afflicting these nations. This has prompted scholars and researchers to revisit African traditional practices and their relevance in a post-colonial state (Ndiaye, 2012). Although indigenous justice systems are not flawless, discarding them entirely in favor of Western justice models risks not only erasing the cultural practices of indigenous populations but also perpetuates the denigration of African ideas and values, portraying them as inferior to Western values.

Therefore, the concept of restorative justice has historical roots in biblical teachings, particularly evident in various passages that emphasize reconciliation, forgiveness, and the restoration of relationships. Here are some Bible verses that highlight the historical perspective of restorative justice:

1. Forgiveness and Reconciliation:

- Matthew 6:14-15 (NIV): "For if you forgive other people when they sin against you, your heavenly Father will also forgive you. But if you do not forgive others their sins, your Father will not forgive your sins."

- Colossians 3:13 (NIV): "Bear with each other and forgive one another if any of you has a grievance against someone. Forgive as the Lord forgave you."

2. Restitution and Repair:

- Exodus 22:1-3 (NIV): "Anyone who steals must certainly make restitution, but if they have nothing, they must be sold to pay for their theft. If the stolen animal is found alive in their possession—whether ox or donkey or sheep—they must pay back double."

- Luke 19:8-9 (NIV): "But Zacchaeus stood up and said to the Lord, 'Look, Lord! Here and now I give half of my possessions to the poor, and if I have cheated anybody out of anything, I will pay back four times the amount.'"

3. Reconciliation and Healing:

- Matthew 5:23-24 (NIV): "Therefore, if you are offering your gift at the altar and there remember that your brother or sister has something against you, leave your gift there in front of the altar. First go and be reconciled to them; then come and offer your gift."

- James 5:16 (NIV): "Therefore confess your sins to each other and pray for each other so that you may be healed. The prayer of a righteous person is powerful and effective."

4. Justice and Compassion:

- Micah 6:8 (NIV): "He has shown you, O mortal, what is good. And what does the Lord require of you? To act justly and to love mercy and to walk humbly with your God."

- Isaiah 1:17 (NIV): "Learn to do right; seek justice. Defend the oppressed. Take up the cause of the fatherless; plead the case of the widow."

These verses reflect the biblical principles of resolving conflicts, seeking restitution, and fostering reconciliation—a foundation that aligns with the essence of restorative justice. The Bible emphasizes the transformative power of forgiveness, restitution, and reconciliation in the context of justice and community relationships.

Retributive Justice

Retributive justice is a system of criminal justice that focuses solely on punishment of law breakers and the compensation of victims, in contrast, the deterrence—prevention of future crimes—or the rehabilitation of offenders. In general, retributive justice is based on the principle that the severity of the punishment should be in proportion to the seriousness of the crime committed.

Retribution is simultaneously with restorative principles in law codes from the ancient Near East, including the Code of Ur-Nammu (c. 2050 BC) [The Code of Ur-Nammu is the oldest known law code surviving today. It is from Mesopotamia and is written on tablets, in the Sumerian language c. 2100–2050 BC], the Laws of Eshnunna (c. 2000 BC) [The Laws of Eshnunna (abrv. LE) are inscribed on two cuneiform tablets discovered in Tell Abū Harmal, Baghdad, Iraq. The Iraqi Directorate of Antiquities headed by Taha Baqir unearthed two parallel sets of tablets in 1945 and 1947. The two tablets are separate copies of an older source and date back to ca. 1930 BC], and the better-known Babylonian Code of Hammurabi (c. 1750 BC) [The Code of Hammurabi is a Babylonian legal text composed c. 1755–1750 BC. It is the longest, best-organized, and best-preserved legal text from the ancient Near East. It is written in the Old Babylonian dialect of Akkadian, purportedly by Hammurabi, sixth king of the First Dynasty of Babylon]. In those legal systems, collectively referred to as cuneiform law, crimes were considered violations of other people's rights. Victims were to be compensated for the intentional and unintentional harms they suffered, and offenders were to be punished because they had done wrong.

Retribution is based on the concept of the law of retaliation known as lex talionis. At its core is the principle of equal and direct retribution, as impeccably exhibited in [Exodus 21:24 eye for eye, tooth for tooth, hand for hand, foot for foot,] as "an eye for an eye." Destroying the tooth of a person of equal social standing meant that one's own tooth would be removed, inter-alia, destroying the eye of a person of equal social standing meant that one's own eye would be put out, to wit. Some penalties designed to punish culpable behavior by individuals were specifically tied to outlawed acts. Branders who used their skills to remove slave marks from runaway slaves, for example, had their hands amputated.

While an abstract idea of retribution dates way back to pre-biblical times, consequently, retributive justice has played a major role in current thinking about the punishment of lawbreakers, the ultimate justification for it remains contested and problematic.

Theory and Principles of Retributive Justice

Retributive justice is founded on the theorem that when an individual commits a crime, "justice" requires that he/she be punished in return and that the severity of his/her punishment should be proportionate to the solemnity of their crime.

While the idea, theorem, method, or the concept has been used in a variety of ways, retributive justice is best recognized as that form of justice committed to the following three principles:

- Those who commit crimes–especially serious crimes—morally deserve to suffer a proportionate punishment.
- The punishment should be determined and applied by officials of a legitimate criminal justice system.
- It is morally impermissible to intentionally punish the innocent or to inflict disproportionately harsh punishments on wrongdoers.

Disengaging it from sheer revenge, retributive justice should not be personal. In contrast, it is administered only at the wrongdoing involved, has inherent limits, seeks no pleasure from the suffering of wrongdoers, and employs clearly defined procedural standards.

Pursuant to the fundamental's truth, propositions and practices of procedural and substantive law the government through prosecution before a judge must establish the guilt of a person for violation of the law. Following the determination of guilt, a judge imposes the appropriate sentence, which can include a fine, probation, imprisonment, and in extreme cases, the death penalty.

Consequently, retributive justice is to be executed swiftly and must cost the lawbreaker something, which does not include the collateral consequences of the crime, such as the pain of emotional trauma and suffering of the malefactor's family.

Retribution of offenders also serves to restore balance to community or society by gratifying the public's desire for vengeance. The transgressors are considered to have misused society's benefits and have thus gained an unethical advantage over their law-abiding counterparts. Retributive which is contrast to restorative punishment, removes that advantage and tries to restore balance to society by validating how individuals ought to behave in society. Punishing wrongdoers for their crimes also reminds others in the public that such conduct is inappropriate for law-abiding citizens, thus helping to deter further wrongdoing.

Historic Context

The concept and theorem of retribution appears in the ancient codes of laws from the ancient Near East, including the Babylonian Code of Hammurabi from around 1750 BCE. In this and other ancient legal systems, collectively referred to as cuneiform law, crimes were considered to have violated other people's rights. Victims were to be compensated for the intentional and unintentional harms they suffered, and offenders were to be punished because they had done wrong.

King Hammurabi was an important Babylonian king known best for an early law code, that we refer to by his name. He united Mesopotamia and turned Babylonia into an important power. Some refer to Hammurabi as Hammurapi

Code of Hammurabi

Hammurabi is now synonymous with his code of laws, referred to as the Code of Hammurabi. Five columns of the stele on which his laws were written (inscribed) have been erased. Scholars estimate the total number of legal judgments contained on the stele when it was intact would have been around 300.

The stele may not actually contain laws, per se, as judgments made by Hammurabi. By recording the judgments, he made, the stele would have served to testify to and honor King Hammurabi's acts and deeds.

Hammurabi and the Bible

Hammurabi may have been the Biblical Amraphel, King of Sennaar, mentioned in the Bible book of Genesis.

Hammurabi Dates

Hammurabi was the sixth king of the First Babylonian dynasty -- about 4000 years ago. We don't know for sure when -- during a general period running from 2342 to 1050 B.C. -- he ruled, but the standard Middle Chronology puts his dates at 1792-1750. (Put that date in context by looking at the major events timeline.) [Source] King Hammurabi of Babylonia - Biographical Profile (thoughtco.com)

As a philosophy of justice, retribution recurs in many religious sects. There are mentions of it in several religious texts, including the Infallible Word, Bible. Adam and Eve, for example, were cast out of the Garden of Eden because they violated God's rules of not eating fruit of knowledge of good and evil, and thus deserved to be punished. In the Pentateuch, the Torahic law, Exodus 21:24 direct retribution is expressed as "an eye for an eye, "an eye for an eye, a tooth for a tooth." Plucking out the eye of a person of equal social standing meant that one's own eye would be put out. Some penalties designed to punish culpable behavior by individuals were specifically tied to outlawed acts. Thieves, for example, had their hands amputated.

The German philosopher and Central Enlightenment thinker Immanuel Kant, in the 18th century developed a theory of retribution based on logic and reason. In Kant's observations and reckoning, the only purpose punishment should serve is to penalize the lawbreakers for committing a crime. To Kant, the punishment's effect on the criminal's likelihood of being rehabilitated is irrelevant, which is the main purpose of restorative justice, "restoration". The punishment is there to punish the lawbreakers for the crime they have committed—nothing more, nothing less. Kant's theories created, coupled with the very nature of retributive justice fueled the arguments of Kant's modern critics who argue that his approach would lead to harsh and ineffective sentencing. The Gospel of Matthew quotes Isaiah 7:14: "'The virgin will be with child and will give birth to a son, and they will call him

Immanuel'—which means, 'God with us'" (Matthew 1:23 NIV). Although philosopher Immanuel Kant (1724–1804) bore the name meaning "God with us," his ideas resulted in skepticism that places God beyond us.

Kant's views led to the theory of "just deserts," or the now more prominent views on the subject of the punishment of criminals that offenders must deserve to be punished. Ask people on the street why criminals should be punished, and most of them are likely to say "because they 'deserve' it."

Being discerning of philosophy requires some level of familiarity and understanding of it. Moreover, not all philosophy is "bad". "Good philosophy must exist, if for no other reason, because bad philosophy needs to be answered." Learning to interact with, and respond intelligently to, philosophical ideas is part of the Christian calling to love God with all of our minds and to defend the faith (see Matthew 22:37 Jesus replied: "'Love the Lord your God with all your heart and with all your soul and with all your mind and 1 Peter 3:15 But in your hearts revere Christ as Lord. Always be prepared to give an answer to everyone who asks you to give the reason for the hope that you have. But do this with gentleness and respect).

Philosophy is the "love of wisdom." Wisdom includes the ability to make correct judgments based on a proper understanding of reality. Any thoughtful study of philosophy requires familiarity with the basic terms of the discipline. Three questions summarize main areas of philosophical study: (1) What is ultimate reality? (2) How do we know? and (3) How should this knowledge of ultimate reality guide our conduct?

Philosopher Kant goes on to suggest that adhering to the law is a sacrifice of one's right to freedom of choice. Therefore, those that break the laws gain an unfair advantage over those that do not. Punishment, therefore, is necessary as a means to rectify the balance between the law-abiding citizens and the criminals, removing any unfairly gained advantage from the criminals.

Many legal scholars argue that widespread adoption of Kant's theories has resulted in a trend of modern criminal justice systems to criminalize too much conduct, such as the simple possession of small amounts of marijuana, and to punish those conducts too severely—or to "over-prosecute" and "over-sentence."

Today, unification of the current system of retributive justice, with a recently developed approach of restorative justice has shown promise in reducing the harshness of contemporary sentencing while also providing meaningful relief to crime victims. Restorative justice seeks to evaluate the harmful impact of a crime on its victims and determine what can be done to best repair that harm while holding the person or persons who caused it accountable for their actions. Through organized face-to-face meetings among all parties connected to a crime, the goal of restorative justice is to reach an agreement on what the offender can do to repair the harm caused by their offense rather than simply handing out punishment. Critics of such an approach argue that it can create conflicts between the reconciliation objective of restorative justice and the condemnatory objective of retributive punishment.

Prisons were originally promoted as a humane alternative to corporal and capital punishment.

For most of history, imprisoning was not a punishment in itself, but rather a way to confine criminals until corporal or capital punishment was administered. Only in the 19th century, beginning in Britain, did prisons as known today become commonplace.

There are two types of people in jail or prison: those who were wrongfully accused and victimized by an unjust system, and those who are guilty and whose punishment is just according to the system of law they have broken. The Bible has something to say to both the innocent and guilty who are in jail/prison. To the guilty, the Bible recommends truth and submission to the laws of the government, and it offers freedom from the spiritual prison of sin—freedom that comes through the person of Christ – Romans 6:18. To the innocent and wrongfully accused, the Bible offers peace, patience, and hope in difficult circumstances, as well as the hope of heavenly reward.

Pursuant to Encyclopedias – International Standard Bible Encyclopedia, Prison or prisoner is priz'-n, priz'-'-n-er, priz'-ner (there are various Hebrew words which are rendered "prison" in the King James Version, among them:
1. Hebrew Words:

(1) cohar, "round house," "fortress" (8 times in Genesis), (2) kele' "restraint," "confinement" (12 times: in historic books, Isaiah, Jeremiah, with "house"), (3) maTTarah, "guard," "sentry" (13 times in Jeremiah and Nehemiah), (4) mahaphekheth, "distorting," i.e., stocks or pillory (4 times), (5) 'ecur, "bond," "fetters" Ecclesiastes 4:14 and Jeremiah 37:15); "ward" in the King James Version is usually the rendering for mishmar):

2. In Early Times:

The earliest occurrence of the word "prison" in the King James Version is found in the narrative of Joseph's life in Egypt (the Jahwist). The term used, namely, cohar, means perhaps "round house" or "tower." It seems probable that among the Hebrews there were no special buildings erected as "jails" in the premonarchical period, and perhaps not before the post-exilic period, when the adoption of the civic institutions and customs of surrounding nations prevailed. In Egypt and Assyria, on the contrary, there were probably public buildings corresponding to our modern jails. Among the Hebrews, rooms in connection with the royal palace or the residence of prominent court officials would be used for the purpose.

3. Joseph in Egypt:

According to one narrative (Jahwist) in Genesis the prison in which Joseph was confined had a "keeper," while according to another narrative (the Elohist) the offending members of the royal household, namely, the royal butler and the royal baker, were placed "in ward" with the "captain of the guard" in charge, i.e., in some part of the royal palace. This is still more probable if, instead of "captain of the guard," we should translate "chief of the cooks" i.e., superintendent of the royal kitchen.

4. Causes of Imprisonment:

It was often necessary to restrict the liberty of individuals who for various causes were a menace to those in authority, without inflicting any corporal punishment, e.g. Joseph's brethren were kept "in ward" three days - Genesis 42:19; Shimei was forbidden to pass beyond the boundary of Jerusalem - 1 Kings 2:36; the person who was caught gathering sticks on the Sabbath was put "in ward" pending his trial - Numbers 15:34. In the monarchical period, prophets who criticized the throne were put in prison, e.g. Micaiah by Ahab – 1 Kings 22:27, Hanani by Asa – 2 Chronicles 16:10. Hoshea, after his abortive effort to institute an alliance with So or Seve, king of Egypt, was shut up in prison by Shalmaneser - 2 Kings 17:4; compare also – 2 Kings 25:27 (Jehoiachin in Babylon); - Jeremiah 52:11 (Zedekiah in Babylon).

5. Under the Monarchy:

The Book of Jeremiah throws considerable light on the prison system of Jerusalem in the later monarchical period. The prophet was put "in the stocks that were in the upper gate of Benjamin, which was in the house of Yahweh" (20:2). Mere imprisonment was not adequate punishment for the prophet's announcement of Judah's doom; it was necessary to have recourse to the pillory. During the siege of Jerusalem Jeremiah was confined in the "court of the guard, which was in the king of Judah's house" (32:2, etc.). The "court of the guard" was the quarters of the sentry who guarded the royal palace. According to the narrative of Jeremiah 37, the prophet was arrested on a charge of treachery and put in prison "in the house of Jonathan the scribe" (37:15). This verse does not necessarily mean that a private house was used as a prison. The words are capable of another interpretation, namely, that a building known as the "house of Jonathan the Scribe" had been taken over by the authorities and converted into a jail. We read in the following verse that the house had a "dungeon" (literally, "house of the pit") and "cabins" or "cells."

6. The Treatment of Prisoners:

The data are not sufficient to enable us to give any detailed description of the treatment of prisoners. This treatment varied according to the character of the offense which led to incarceration. Samson during the period of his imprisonment was compelled to do hard labor Judges 16:21. Grinding was the occupation of women, and marked the depth of Samson's humiliation. Dangerous persons were subjected to various kinds of physical mutilation, e.g., Samson was deprived of his sight. This was a common practice in Assyria - 2 Kings 25:7. The thumbs and great toes of Adonibezek were cut off to render him incapable of further resistance Judges 1:6.

Various forms of torture were in vogue. Hanani the seer was put into the pillory by Asa (for "in a prison house" we should render "in the stocks"; see the Revised Version margin). In Jeremiah 29:26 for "prison," we should render "stocks" (so the Revised

Version (British and American)) or "pillory," and for "stocks," "collar" (as in the Revised Version margin). the King James Version renders a different Hebrew word by "stocks" in Job (13:27; 33:11). There was a special prison diet 1 Kings 22:27, as well as a prison garb 2 Kings 25:29.

7. Other Hebrew Words:

There are other Hebrew words rendered "prison" (sometimes incorrectly) in the King James Version. In Psalms 142:7, the word which is translated as "prison" means a "place of execution," and is derived from a root that denotes, for instance, the isolation of the leper Leviticus 13:5; compare 24:22; 42:7). In Isaiah 53:8 "oppression" not "prison" is the correct translation while in Isaiah 61:1 the Hebrew denotes "opening of the eyes," rather than "opening of the prison." Prisoners are promised "light after darkness, gleam after gloom."

8. In the New Testament:

In the New Testament "prison" generally occurs for the Greek word phulake, which corresponds to the Hebrew word mishmar, referred to above (Matthews 5:25; Mark 6:17; Luke 3:20; Acts 5:19; 1 Peter 3:19), the King James Version renders this word by two different words, namely, "hold" and "cage"; the Revised Version (British and American) employs "hold" in each case (the Revised Version margin "prison"). In one passage "ward" is the rendering in the King James Version - Acts 12:10. In connection with the imprisonment of John the term used is desmoterion, "place of bonds" or "fetters" – Matthew 11:2; the same word is used in the case of Peter and John – Acts 5:21,23, and of Paul and Silas – Acts 16:26. But the more common term is also found in these narratives. In Acts 12:17 "prison" renders a Greek word which means "dwelling." In Acts 5:18 the King James Version, "prison" is the rendering for another Greek word, namely, teresis, "watching" or "ward" (the Revised Version (British and American) "ward"). In Acts 4:3, the King James Version employs "hold" as the rendering for the same word. This would correspond to the modern "police station" or "lockup."

Prison "alternatives" have expanded, and the "net" of control and intervention has widened

a) but without discernible effects on crime and
b) and without meeting essential needs of victim or offender.

Because the state and federal governments set standards for sentencing, there is no uniformity from courtroom to courtroom, and from judge to judge, in handing down sentences for the same crime.

When we identify something as a crime, a number of basic assumptions shape our responses.

What do we assume?

a): Guilt must be assigned.

b): The guilty must get their "just deserts."

c): Just deserts require the infliction of pain.

d): Justice is measured by the process.

e): The breaking of the law defines the offense.

The question of guilt is the hub of the entire criminal justice process.

Why are there such elaborate rules governing how to legally establish guilt?

There are elaborate rules governing how to legally establish guilt for several reasons:

1. Protecting the Rights of the Accused: The rules governing the legal establishment of guilt are designed to protect the rights of the accused, ensuring that they are not wrongfully convicted or punished for a crime they did not commit. This includes protections such as the presumption of innocence, the right to a fair trial, and the right to an attorney.

2. Ensuring Fairness and Impartiality: The rules governing the legal establishment of guilt are also designed to ensure fairness and impartiality in the criminal justice system. This includes rules such as the exclusion of evidence obtained through illegal means, the requirement of a unanimous jury verdict in criminal cases, and the requirement of a high standard of proof (beyond a reasonable doubt) to establish guilt.

3. Protecting Against Abuse of Power: The rules governing the legal establishment of guilt are also designed to protect against abuse of power by law enforcement and other authorities. This includes rules such as the requirement of a warrant or probable cause for searches and seizures, and the

requirement of Miranda warnings to inform suspects of their rights.

4. Maintaining Public Confidence in the Justice System: The rules governing the legal establishment of guilt are also important for maintaining public confidence in the justice system. When the rules are followed and a fair trial is conducted, it helps to ensure that the public perceives the outcome as just and legitimate, which is essential for the functioning of a democratic society.

Hence, the rules governing the legal establishment of guilt are an essential component of the criminal justice system, designed to protect the rights of the accused, ensure fairness and impartiality, prevent abuse of power, and maintain public confidence in the justice system.

Wherefore, once guilt has been established, concern about procedural safeguards and rights diminishes.

Even is a person is declared "not guilty," consequences are profound. Accused persons go to trial based on evidence presented by the police, although in some cases haphazardly. It seems to most that the accused is more than likely guilty of the crime alleged. After all, the district attorney must have had quite a load of proof on hand before making the decision to prosecute. A terrible stain is already cast upon a person. Even if the jury concludes that reasonable doubt exists as to guilt, this is an accusation that will be with that person for life.

The concept of guilt which guides the justice process is a narrow, highly technical one which is primarily objective or descriptive in nature.

In the legal system, offenses and questions of guilt are framed in terms much different from how the victim and the offender actually experience them.

a) The legal charge may seem to bear little relationship to the actual offense,

b) and the language of guilt or innocence may seem to have little connection to what actually happened.

When the legal charge sounds quite different from the actual offense, and the offender has been advised to plead "not guilty," many times the offender comes to believe that he is in fact not guilty.

In legal terms, what does the plea "not guilty" actually mean?

Is the way one says, "I want a trial," or "I need more time."

Social and behavioral scientists raise questions about the extent to which the offender is personally responsible, perhaps about the extent to which he is an offender rather than a victim.

Wherefore, the label of "guilty" sticks to a person for his entire life, and does become a part of his/her identity.

In Western culture, the basic assumption of human freedom and of personal accountability is important:

Even though the Apostle Paul confirmed that we have free will and the freedom to make choices, he also lamented that the power of evil can have a strong pull on our will and get us into trouble. In Romans 7:15, he said:

a) vs. 15a: I do not understand what I do.

b) vs. 15b: For what I want to do I do not do,

c) vs. 15c: but what I hate I do.

The Apostle Paul's problem isn't knowledge - he knows what the right thing is. His problem is a lack of power, how to do the right thing. He lacks power because the law gives no power.

In the very last days of Moses' life, when he was 120 years old, he made his farewell speech to the nation of Israel. Regarding the matter of free choice, what did Moses say are our two choices? (Deuteronomy 30:15):

a): See, I set before you today life and prosperity,

b): Death and destruction.

Israel had a choice: life or death, good or evil. It was up to them. God was going to glorify Himself through Israel one way or another. How it would happen was really their choice. It is still the same for us today.

Joshua took over as leader of Israel after the death of Moses, and in the final days of his life he too spoke about this matter of free choice. In Joshua 24:15, what did Joshua say were the two choices.:

a): Then choose for yourselves this day whom you will serve, whether the gods your ancestors served beyond the Euphrates, b): Or the gods of the Amorites, in whose land you are living.

What choice did Joshua make for himself and his family?

But as for me and my household, we will serve the Lord."

Joshua's bold statement indicates that he was determined to follow this course no matter what anyone else thought. His relationship with God was not based on any man, but on the Lord alone, and he would serve God no matter what anyone else thought or did.

a) Do you believe offenders should be held accountable for what they have done, regardless of background or circumstances, or do you believe we should take into consideration the social and economic roots and contexts of the crime as well.

Take into consideration the social and economic roots and contexts of the crime

b) Individuals background has an impact in one's decision, and we should not condemn them without knowing their back ground which may be the force to their wrong choices. Example, A person who was raised in a violent environment may be violent when he grows up.

I believe that every action that we take is accountable to some law whether it is the law of gravity, or a law of decency, or a law of the criminal justice system. If we cause harm to someone else or to someone's property, we should be held accountable for our actions.

The criminal justice system and our court systems were created to enforce the laws of accountability and responsibility. For those who refuse to be accountable, I believe these should be dealt with more severely.

In what way does the legal process discourage offenders from being accountable for or accepting responsibility for the choices between good and evil they have made? (Thought question - answers will vary.):

By giving them an option of making a not guilty plea. This makes and offender feels and believe in fact he/she is not guilt.

Being accountable for our own actions means that we would take responsibility for the outcome. If we were to jump off of a high wall, we would be accountable to ourselves for the fact that the laws of gravity will take over and bring us to the ground. If we act in a way that affects others, we must be held accountable for the effect that our actions had on them. However, many try to shift blame on to the parents, environment, mental illness, society etc.

Once guilt has been established, what is the second assumption that comes into play?

We assume that offenders must receive their "just deserts."

Just deserts, in the sense of "things deserved" has been used in the English language since at least the 13th century. Originally, it meant to get a reward for what had been done - whether good or bad. Similarly, "Let the punishment fit the crime" is a principle that means the severity of penalty for a misdeed or wrongdoing should be reasonable and proportionate to the severity of the infraction. The concept is common to most cultures throughout the world.

Criminal justice officials see their job as meting out appropriate levels of punishment.

What are a few of the rationales for delivering pain to the offender?

a): Pain. At some times we have done it in the name of treatment, as a means of rehabilitation.

b): Consequences. We administer pain in the name of deterrence, in fact, despite substantial questions about whether such deterrence actually works.

c): We administer pain in the name of deterrence despite questions about the morality of administering pain to one person for the purposes of possibly deterring another.

Because of this focus on inflicting pain, because of the threat of punishment, and because the punitive consequences are so serious:

a): elaborate safeguards of offenders' right are needed,

b): and these can make it difficult to get at truth.

c): Judges and jurors too may become less likely to convict when the potential punishment is seen as very severe.

Usually, the jury decides the facts of a case, but the judge determines the punishment. Some have suggested that judges alone should determine guilt in all cases. Juries are not technically trained in evaluating evidence. Additionally, judges are trained to recognize and suppress their own prejudices, evaluate information given to them, recognize prosecutorial strategy etc.

Studies of capital punishment have proven that the death penalty does not deters people from killing.

The threat to inflict pain on those who disobey has long been recognized as ...: basis of modern law.

The primary goal of our justice process is first the determination of guilt and once that is determined, the infliction of pain.

Appeals are usually centered on whether correct procedures have been followed.

With this emphasis on rules and process, priority is given to equity of treatment as a test of justice.

Due to stringent rules and regulations in the legal process, approximate equity in outcome is usually not achieved.

The criminal judicial system has become a huge bureaucracy with vested of its own.

What actually defines the offense and triggers the justice process?

The act of breaking a law, not the damage or conflict,

What weight or importance is given to social, moral, or personal factors?

Moral and social issues

Studies about the influence of economic factors on criminal behavior have attempted to link being financially deprived to increased motivation to commit crimes (especially property crimes). Other studies attempt to relate the involvement of criminals from poor neighborhoods to the distribution of power in society. The assumption in these studies is that criminal law is a tool used by the rich to advance their class interests. Studies of the relationship between unemployment and crime have also been used to explain away or excuse crime.

However, whatever the excuse or rationale, I believe a criminal should be accountable for his/her actions.

What are the five assumptions that we make about crime and justice?

There are many assumptions made about crime and justice, but five common ones are:

1. Crime is a violation of the law: This assumption states that crime is not just a violation of moral principles, but also a

violation of a specific law or legal code that is designed to protect society from harmful behavior.

2. Crime is a rational choice: This assumption assumes that individuals who engage in criminal behavior do so after weighing the costs and benefits of their actions and deciding that the benefits outweigh the risks.

3. The justice system is impartial: This assumption assumes that the justice system is impartial and objective, and that it treats all individuals fairly and equally under the law.

4. Punishment deters crime: This assumption assumes that punishment, such as imprisonment or fines, deters individuals from committing future crimes by making them fear the consequences of their actions.

5. The justice system rehabilitates offenders: This assumption assumes that the justice system can rehabilitate offenders and help them change their behavior through programs such as counseling, education, and vocational training.

It is important to note that these assumptions are not always true in every case and that they have been subject to criticism and debate in the field of criminology.

a): Crime is essentially lawbreaking;

b): When a law is broken, justice involves establishing guilt;

c): So that just deserts can be meted out;

d): By inflicting pain;

e): through a conflict in which rules and intentions are placed above outcomes.

In criminal law, who is defined as the victim?

The State

Therefore, criminal law pits offenders against the State

Why are safeguards for the procedures so essential?

Because the state is so impersonal and abstract, forgiveness and mercy are nearly impossible to achieve.

Within our criminal justice system, why are forgiveness and mercy nearly impossible to achieve?

Because the state is so impersonal and abstract, forgiveness and mercy are nearly impossible to achieve.

Why doesn't the justice process include seeking reconciliation between the victim and the offender?

Because the relationship between victim and offender is not seen as an important problem.

This author contends that ours is essentially a retributive model of justice, and that model is at the root of many of our problems.

The idea that we should treat people as they deserve is commonly accepted. We do not think that war criminals should be allowed to live carefree lives after committing unspeakable crimes against humanity. However, there is a dangerous tendency to slip from retributive justice to an emphasis on revenge.

Sources:

Wharton, Francis. "Retributive Justice." Franklin Classics, October 16, 2018, ISBN-10: 0343579170.

Contini, Cory. "The Transition from Retributive to Transformative Justice: Transforming the System of Justice." GRIN Publishing, July 25, 2013, ISBN-10: 3656462275.

Husak, Douglas. "Overcriminalization: The Limits of the Criminal Law." Oxford University Press ,November 30, 2009, ISBN-10: 0195399013.

Aston, Joseph. "Retributive Justice: A Tragedy." Palala Press, May 21, 2016, ISBN-10: 1358425558.

Hermann, Donald H.J. "Restorative Justice and Retributive Justice." Seattle Journal for Social Justice, 12-19-2017, https://digitalcommons.law.seattleu.edu/cgi/viewcontent.cgi?article=1889&context=sjsj.

CHAPTER 07

MODERN RESTORATIVE JUSTICE

Modern restorative justice is a contemporary approach to addressing harm, conflicts, and crimes that focuses on repairing the harm done to victims, reintegrating offenders into society, and involving the community in the resolution process. This approach has gained significant attention in recent years and is widely regarded as a more humane and effective alternative to punitive justice systems. Here are key features of modern restorative justice:

1. Victim-Centered: Modern restorative justice places victims at the center of the process. It seeks to meet their needs, provide opportunities for them to express their feelings and concerns, and offer a role in shaping the resolution.

2. Offender Accountability: While emphasizing accountability, modern restorative justice takes a more rehabilitative approach. Offenders are encouraged to take responsibility for their actions, understand the harm they've caused, and actively participate in making amends.

3. Community Involvement: It involves the community in the justice process. Community members can serve as mediators, support networks for victims and offenders, and participants in decision-making circles.

4. Resolution and Healing: Modern restorative justice aims to achieve resolution and healing rather than just punishment. It

prioritizes the restoration of relationships and the repair of harm, which is often missing in punitive systems.

5. Diverse Applications: Restorative justice is applied not only in criminal justice but also in education, family and community disputes, workplace conflicts, and other areas of social life. It offers a versatile framework for resolving various types of conflicts.

6. Structured Processes: Restorative justice often follows structured processes such as victim-offender mediation, family group conferences, and circles. These processes guide the parties involved in addressing the harm and finding appropriate solutions.

7. Evidence-Based Success: Research has shown that restorative justice programs can reduce recidivism rates, improve victim satisfaction, and offer a cost-effective alternative to traditional punitive approaches.

8. Global Reach: Modern restorative justice is not limited to one geographic region; it has been implemented in various countries and cultures, adapting to local contexts while maintaining core principles.

Overall, modern restorative justice offers a more balanced and compassionate approach to addressing wrongdoing. It aligns with the teachings of Jesus and biblical principles of forgiveness, reconciliation, and redemption, making it a promising framework for promoting justice and healing in contemporary society.

Our current criminal justice system works on a premise that largely ignores the rehabilitation of the offender, the victim, and the community that is hurt most by the crime.

There is a growing recognition that the current criminal justice system often fails to prioritize rehabilitation and restoration for the offender, victim, and community. Instead, the focus has traditionally been on punishment and retribution.

This approach to justice can be seen as problematic because it fails to address the underlying causes of criminal behavior and does little to prevent recidivism. Punishment alone is often not enough to deter offenders from committing further crimes, and it may actually contribute to a cycle of criminal behavior by exacerbating the social, economic, and psychological factors that can lead to criminal activity.

Moreover, the current criminal justice system often neglects the needs and perspectives of victims and communities affected by crime. Victims may feel isolated and powerless in the face of the justice system, and communities may experience a loss of trust in law enforcement and the broader justice system.

In contrast, restorative and community justice approaches prioritize rehabilitation and restoration for all stakeholders. These approaches recognize the importance of addressing the underlying causes of criminal behavior and promoting healing and restoration for victims and communities. They also emphasize the importance of involving all stakeholders in the justice process and building stronger relationships between law enforcement and the community.

Consequently, while the current criminal justice system serves an important role in holding offenders accountable for their actions, there is a growing recognition that it must also prioritize rehabilitation, restoration, and community engagement to promote long-term public safety and prevent recidivism.

What is the primary focus of today's criminal justice system?

The primary focus of today's criminal justice system is often seen as punishing offenders for their crimes. While this is an important aspect of the justice system, critics argue that the system often fails to address the underlying causes of criminal behavior and does little to help offenders face the impact of their crimes.

Under the current system, offenders are typically punished through incarceration, fines, or other forms of legal penalties. While these penalties can serve as a deterrent for future criminal behavior, they may not address the underlying issues that led to the crime in the first place. Additionally, the current system may not offer enough support for offenders to reintegrate into society once their sentence is completed, which can lead to recidivism and further criminal behavior.

Moreover, the current criminal justice system may not adequately address the impact of the crime on victims and communities. Victims may feel ignored or disrespected by the justice system, and communities may feel a lack of trust in law enforcement and the broader justice system.

In contrast, restorative and community justice approaches prioritize rehabilitation and restoration for all stakeholders. These approaches recognize the importance of addressing the underlying causes of criminal behavior and promoting healing and restoration for victims and communities. They also emphasize the importance of involving all stakeholders in the justice process and building stronger relationships between law enforcement and the community.

Accordingly, while the current criminal justice system serves an important role in holding offenders accountable for their actions, there is a growing recognition that it must also prioritize rehabilitation, restoration, and community engagement to promote long-term public safety and prevent recidivism.

Note: This is very true. Many years ago, Texas prisons were called the Texas Department of Corrections. They were supposed to rehabilitate the offender. However, this was not the case and an offender successfully sued the State over the matter. As a result, the prison system is now called the Texas Department of Criminal Justice. This system punishes the offender without helping them face the impact of their crimes.

The restorative justice principles offer more inclusive processes and reorient the goals of justice.

The principles of restorative justice offer a more inclusive and community-oriented approach to justice. Restorative justice focuses on repairing harm caused by crime by involving all stakeholders in the process of addressing the harm and preventing future harm. The goals of restorative justice include not only holding offenders accountable for their actions but also promoting healing and restoration for victims and communities, and addressing the underlying causes of criminal behavior.

Restorative justice principles include:

1. Focus on harm: Restorative justice prioritizes repairing the harm caused by crime, rather than punishing offenders.
2. Inclusivity: Restorative justice involves all stakeholders in the justice process, including victims, offenders, and communities.
3. Empowerment: Restorative justice seeks to empower victims and communities by giving them a voice in the

justice process and by allowing them to play an active role in the resolution of the harm caused by the crime.

4. Collaboration: Restorative justice emphasizes collaboration and problem-solving, with the goal of finding solutions that are satisfactory to all stakeholders.

5. Accountability: Restorative justice holds offenders accountable for their actions while providing them with opportunities for rehabilitation and reintegration into society.

Thence, the principles of restorative justice offer a more inclusive, collaborative, and community-oriented approach to justice that seeks to promote healing and restoration for victims and communities, while also addressing the underlying causes of criminal behavior.

Note: The primary stakeholders in the restorative justice process are the person who caused the harm (the offender), the person harmed (the victim), and the affected community. It is the goal of restorative justice to create healing by identifying and addressing the harms, needs, and obligations that result from wrongdoing.

Why has restorative justice been finding a receptive audience?

"Because it creates common ground which accommodates the goals of many constituencies and provides a collective focus."

Restorative justice has been finding a receptive audience because it offers a more inclusive and collaborative approach to justice that accommodates the goals of many constituencies and provides a collective focus.

Restorative justice seeks to involve all stakeholders in the justice process, including victims, offenders, and communities. By involving these stakeholders in the process of repairing harm caused by crime, restorative justice promotes healing and restoration for victims and communities, while also holding offenders accountable for their actions. This collaborative approach to justice creates common ground among stakeholders and can build stronger relationships between law enforcement and the community.

Additionally, restorative justice prioritizes addressing the underlying causes of criminal behavior, which can help to prevent future crime and promote long-term public safety. By focusing on rehabilitation and reintegration, restorative justice can help to reduce recidivism rates and improve outcomes for offenders and communities.

Accordingly, restorative justice's emphasis on collaboration, inclusivity, and addressing the root causes of criminal behavior has resonated with many communities and stakeholders who are looking for a more effective and humane approach to justice. By providing a collective focus on repairing harm and promoting healing, restorative justice offers a promising alternative to traditional punitive approaches to justice.

Has restorative justice been recognized by the United States Department of Justice?

This nation-wide trend has been recognized by the United States Department of Justice.

Restorative justice has been recognized by the United States Department of Justice. The Department of Justice has acknowledged the potential benefits of restorative justice and has provided funding and support for restorative justice programs throughout the country.

In 2014, the Department of Justice's Office of Justice Programs launched the National Center for Restorative Justice, which provides training and technical assistance to jurisdictions and organizations seeking to implement restorative justice programs. The Department of Justice has also funded a variety of restorative justice initiatives, including victim-offender mediation programs and community conferencing programs.

Additionally, several states and local jurisdictions have implemented restorative justice programs with the support and encouragement of the Department of Justice. These programs have shown promising results in reducing recidivism rates and improving outcomes for victims and communities.

Therefore, the recognition and support of the Department of Justice have helped to legitimize and promote restorative justice as a viable alternative to traditional punitive approaches to justice in the United States.

Briefly describe community justice.:

A concept that builds on the problem-solving approach of community policing and creates strong linkages between the police, courts, prosecutors, correction systems and the communities they serve.

Community justice is a concept that builds on the problem-solving approach of community policing and creates strong linkages between the police, courts, prosecutors, correction systems, and the communities they serve. It emphasizes collaboration between justice system stakeholders and community members to identify and address the underlying causes of crime and disorder.

Community justice recognizes that crime is often the result of complex social problems, such as poverty, substance abuse, and mental health issues, that cannot be addressed through traditional punitive approaches alone. Instead, it seeks to involve community members in the justice process, encourage community-based problem-solving, and promote the use of alternative approaches to justice, such as diversion programs and restorative justice.

Community justice also emphasizes the importance of cultural competence and responsiveness, recognizing that different communities may have different needs and perspectives regarding justice. By working closely with communities to understand their unique concerns and needs, justice system stakeholders can develop more effective and responsive strategies for addressing crime and promoting public safety.

Therefore, community justice represents a collaborative, community-based approach to justice that seeks to build trust, promote accountability, and address the underlying causes of crime and disorder more holistically and effectively.

Community Justice is a concept that builds on the problem-solving approach of community policing and creates strong linkages between the police and courts, prosecutors, correction systems, and the community they serve.

CHAPTER 08

JESUS AS A MODEL FOR RESTORATIVE JUSTICE

Jesus serves as a compelling model for restorative justice due to the alignment between his teachings and the principles of restorative justice. Here are some ways in which Jesus' life and teachings can be seen as a model for this approach:

1. Compassion and Mercy: Jesus consistently demonstrated compassion and mercy in his interactions with those who had sinned or were marginalized. Restorative justice emphasizes these qualities as it seeks to understand the needs of both victims and offenders.

2. Forgiveness: Jesus' emphasis on forgiveness, as seen in the Lord's Prayer and parables like the Unforgiving Servant, is at the core of restorative justice. Forgiveness is a central element in the process of repairing harm and restoring relationships.

3. Reconciliation: Jesus was a peacemaker and promoted reconciliation. Restorative justice aims to restore relationships between victims and offenders, as well as within the broader community, aligning with Jesus' teachings.

4. Accountability: Jesus held individuals accountable for their actions but also offered them opportunities for redemption. Restorative justice balances accountability with the opportunity for offenders to make amends.

5. Community Involvement: Jesus engaged the community in various ways, including in conflict resolution and healing. Restorative justice actively involves the community, often through processes like circles and conferences.

6. Restoration of Dignity: In his interactions with marginalized individuals, Jesus sought to restore their dignity and sense of self-worth. Restorative justice also values the restoration of the offender's dignity while acknowledging the harm caused.

7. Healing and Transformation: Both Jesus' ministry and restorative justice focus on healing and the transformation of individuals and communities. They recognize that punitive measures often perpetuate cycles of harm, while healing offers a path to redemption.

8. Justice as Love in Action: Jesus' teachings on loving one's neighbor and enemies encapsulate the idea that justice is an expression of love. Restorative justice aims to embody love in action, emphasizing empathy, care, and understanding.

By looking to Jesus as a model for restorative justice, we find a compelling example of how compassion, forgiveness, and reconciliation can guide our approach to justice. His teachings and actions inspire a vision of justice that is grounded in love, empathy, and the restoration of individuals and communities, aligning closely with the principles and practices of restorative justice.

1. In Matthew 25:36 Jesus clearly taught that it is His will for the Church to minister in prison: "I was in prison and you visited Me." This mandate has been reaffirmed in Hebrews 13:3: "Remember them that are in bonds, as bound with them."

The Bible teaches that Christians are called to minister to those who are in prison or in other forms of confinement. In addition to the verses you mentioned, there are many other passages in the Bible that emphasize the importance of caring for prisoners and those who are marginalized or oppressed.

For example, in Isaiah 61:1, the prophet declares that God has anointed him to "preach good tidings unto the meek; he hath sent me to bind up the brokenhearted, to proclaim liberty to the captives, and the opening of the prison to them that are bound." Similarly, in Matthew 5:7, Jesus says, "Blessed are the merciful, for they shall obtain mercy."

Throughout the New Testament, we see examples of Christ's compassion for prisoners and his call to his followers to care for them. For example, in Acts 16, we read about how Paul and Silas were thrown into prison for preaching the gospel. Rather than being discouraged or bitter, they used their time in prison to worship and pray, and their witness led to the conversion of their jailer and his family.

In addition to ministering to prisoners themselves, the Church also has an important role to play in advocating for criminal justice reform and promoting restorative justice practices. The Church can provide a powerful witness to the world by modeling forgiveness, reconciliation, and healing, even in the midst of brokenness and injustice.

2. What are some questions that are raised by the mandate to do criminal justice ministry?

a) Is my view of justice consistent with the biblical view?

b) Does a commitment to restorative justice suggest that I do not support retributive efforts to administer justice?

c) What should be my goal and from what perspective do I view my work within the criminal justice system?

d) Do I preach Jesus only and leave past behavior alone, or do I deal with both behavior and faith, and, in dealing with both, in what sequence do I approach the two?

The mandate to do criminal justice ministry raises several questions, including:

1. What specific actions should the Church take to fulfill this mandate?

2. How can the Church balance its role as a spiritual institution with the practical aspects of criminal justice ministry?

3. How can the Church work collaboratively with the criminal justice system, while also advocating for systemic change?

4. What types of support and resources are necessary for the Church to effectively carry out its mandate?

5. How can the Church ensure that its criminal justice ministry is inclusive and equitable, and does not perpetuate systemic biases or discrimination?

6. How can the Church help to address the root causes of crime, such as poverty, inequality, and lack of access to education and employment opportunities?

7. How can the Church support both victims and offenders in the restorative justice process, while also upholding the principles of accountability and justice?

3. Restorative justice is a Biblical-based paradigm, that is founded in a call to the ministry of reconciliation.

2 Corinthians 5:18 refers to the ministry of reconciliation, assigned to all believers. The message we must declare is that we can have a restored relationship with God through Jesus. The verse says this: "All this is from God, who reconciled us to himself through Christ and gave us the ministry of reconciliation."

Restorative justice is indeed founded on a Biblical-based paradigm that emphasizes the importance of reconciliation, healing, and restoration. The concept of restorative justice is rooted in the biblical principles of forgiveness, mercy, and justice. In the Old Testament, the concept of justice is central to God's character and His relationship with His people. Justice is not only about punishment, but also about restoring relationships, reconciling people to God and each other, and making things right.

In the New Testament, Jesus taught and modeled restorative justice in His interactions with individuals who were considered outcasts by society, such as the woman caught in adultery and the tax collector Zacchaeus. He demonstrated compassion and forgiveness, and He challenged the religious leaders of the time to consider the importance of mercy and grace.

The Apostle Paul also emphasized the importance of reconciliation and restoration in his letters to the early Christian communities. He called on them to forgive one another, to reconcile their differences, and to work together for the common good.

Restorative justice seeks to build on these biblical principles by providing a framework for addressing harm, restoring relationships, and promoting healing and reconciliation. Rather than focusing solely on punishment and retribution, restorative justice encourages offenders to take responsibility for their actions, to make amends for the harm they have caused, and to work toward repairing the harm done to the victim and the community.

In summary, restorative justice is grounded in the biblical call to the ministry of reconciliation, which emphasizes the importance of forgiveness, mercy, and justice in addressing harm and restoring relationships.

4. The ministry of reconciliation requires that we view man through the eyes of Jesus, rather than as the World views him.:

Jesus made the statement (John 3:17) that "God did not send His Son into the world to condemn the world, but that the world through Him might be saved." When He comes again, He will come in judgment upon those who refuse His offer of salvation. Until then, we must remember that mankind is so important to Jesus that He died for them (John 3:16).

The ministry of reconciliation is grounded in the belief that human beings are created in the image of God and that their worth and dignity must be recognized and affirmed. This means that we must view individuals through the eyes of Jesus, who saw them as valuable and worthy of love and redemption, regardless of their past actions.

In contrast, the world often views individuals based on their actions or social status, and can stigmatize and marginalize those who have been involved in the criminal justice system. This can create a cycle of shame and despair that can hinder their ability to make positive changes and reintegrate into society.

The restorative justice paradigm seeks to shift the focus from punishment and retribution to healing and restoration, both for victims and offenders. This requires us to see individuals not just as perpetrators of crime, but as human beings who have the potential to change and be restored to their communities.

By viewing individuals through the eyes of Jesus and embracing the restorative justice paradigm, we can promote healing, reconciliation, and transformation for all those impacted by crime.

5. As a result of his sin, what has Adam passed on to the human race?

"Physical and spiritual death for everyone."

Death has three distinct manifestations: 1) spiritual death or separation from God (Eph. 2:1,2; 4:18); 2) physical death (Heb. 9:27); and 3) eternal death (also known as the second death), which includes not only eternal separation from God, but eternal torment in the lake of fire (Rev. 20:11-15).

In Christian theology, it is believed that as a result of Adam's sin, he passed on the state of sinfulness to all of humanity. This state of sinfulness is commonly referred to as "original sin." The idea of original sin is based on the biblical account in the book of Genesis where Adam and Eve disobeyed God by eating the forbidden fruit from the tree of the knowledge of good and evil.

The concept of original sin teaches that as a result of Adam's disobedience, human nature has been corrupted and inclined towards sin. This means that all human beings are born with a natural tendency towards sin and a predisposition to rebel against God. This sin nature is said to affect every aspect of human life, including thoughts, emotions, and actions.

The Bible teaches that the only way to overcome this state of sinfulness is through faith in Jesus Christ. Through his death and resurrection, Jesus provides a way for human beings to be reconciled to God and to be set free from the power of sin. Restorative justice, therefore, is seen as a means of embodying the ministry of reconciliation by extending forgiveness and restoration to those who have committed offenses, just as Christ has done for us.

6. Although punishment is deserved, Jesus, the Great Mediator between God and man, brings restorative justice to the earth.

Rather than condemn the world "God was in Christ reconciling the world to Himself, not imputing their trespasses to them (2 Corinthians 5:19).

As the Bible teaches, all humans have sinned and fall short of the glory of God (Romans 3:23). The punishment for sin is death (Romans 6:23), but God, in His love and mercy, provided a way for humans to be reconciled to Him through the sacrifice of His son Jesus Christ (John 3:16).

Jesus' death on the cross provided a way for humans to be forgiven of their sins and restored to a right relationship with God. Through faith in Jesus, individuals can receive the forgiveness and reconciliation that He offers (Romans 5:10-11, 2 Corinthians 5:18-19).

In this sense, Jesus brings restorative justice to the earth by reconciling individuals to God and restoring relationships that have been broken by sin. This restorative justice is not limited to the spiritual realm, but can also be extended to the earthly realm through practices such as forgiveness, reconciliation, and restoration. In this way, restorative justice can be seen as an expression of Jesus' love and mercy towards humanity, as well as a way to bring healing and wholeness to broken individuals and communities.

7. The new justice of God is not retributive in nature, but redemptive because:

God's new justice does bring healing because of its redemptive nature. Notice how Paul described God's redemptive justice in Titus 2:14: "Our great God and Savior Jesus Christ, who gave Himself for us, that He might redeem us from every lawless deed and purify for Himself His own special people..."

The concept of restorative justice emphasizes repairing the harm caused by a crime rather than merely punishing the offender. In contrast to traditional retributive justice, which focuses on punishing the offender for breaking the law, restorative justice seeks to restore the harm caused by the offender's actions and promote healing and reconciliation between the offender, victim, and community.

In this sense, the new justice of God is not retributive but redemptive. The Bible teaches that God's justice is rooted in His love and mercy for humanity. Instead of simply punishing humanity for their sins, God seeks to redeem them through His Son Jesus Christ. Through His death and resurrection, Jesus paid the penalty for humanity's sins and offers the gift of salvation to all who repent and believe in Him.

As followers of Christ, we are called to imitate His example of restorative justice. This involves seeking the good of all parties involved, including the offender, victim, and community. Restorative justice recognizes the humanity of all individuals, including those who have committed crimes, and seeks to help them become fully restored members of society. This approach acknowledges that all individuals have inherent value and are capable of change and growth.

In summary, the new justice of God is redemptive, seeking to restore and reconcile all parties involved in a crime. This approach emphasizes love, mercy, and the potential for growth and transformation, rather than punishment and retribution.

8. God's new justice brings healing to relationships with God and the Community of man.

God's new justice, which is restorative in nature, seeks to bring healing and reconciliation to relationships between God and humanity, as well as among people. This is reflected in the life and teachings of Jesus, who taught his followers to love one another, to forgive their enemies, and to seek reconciliation with those they had wronged.

Through Jesus' death and resurrection, he made it possible for humanity to be reconciled to God and to one another. This reconciliation is not simply a matter of forgiving sins and moving on, but of restoring broken relationships and building new ones based on love, trust, and mutual respect.

In this way, restorative justice seeks to bring healing to the harm caused by crime, rather than simply punishing the offender. It recognizes the dignity and worth of every human being and seeks to restore the harm done to the victim, the offender, and the community as a whole.

Restorative justice practices, such as victim-offender mediation and family group conferencing, provide opportunities for those affected by crime to come together, share their experiences, and work towards healing and reconciliation. These practices seek to empower victims, hold offenders accountable, and promote community healing and restoration.

Ultimately, the goal of restorative justice is not simply to punish offenders, but to create a more just and peaceful society, where relationships are characterized by love, forgiveness, and mutual respect, and where harm is transformed into healing and growth.

9. The restorative justice paradigm suggests that crime is an injury to:

The restorative justice paradigm suggests that crime is an injury to God, individuals, relationships, and the community, rather than just a violation of laws and rules. It views crime as harm done to people and relationships, rather than simply as a violation of the state's laws and rules. It emphasizes repairing the harm done to victims and restoring relationships between the offender, victim, and the community, rather than focusing solely on punishing the offender.

In addition, crime causes injury to the criminal him/herself, when you consider all the opportunity costs associated with the criminal's choice to engage in illegal rather than legal and productive activities.

10. What is the goal of restorative justice?

The goal of restorative justice is to repair the harm caused by the crime, promote healing for the victim and community, and hold the offender accountable while giving them an opportunity to make amends and reintegrate into society. It focuses on addressing the root causes of the crime and finding ways to prevent future harm, rather than just punishing the offender. Restorative justice seeks to restore relationships and promote reconciliation between the parties involved, and to empower individuals and communities to take an active role in resolving conflicts and repairing harm.

11. Who accepts the responsibility for the administration of justice in the indigenous communities around the world?

In indigenous communities around the world, the responsibility for the administration of justice is often held by the community itself, rather than by external authorities. This approach to justice is rooted in the community's traditions, values, and cultural practices. Indigenous communities view justice not only as a response to crime or wrongdoing but also as a way of restoring relationships and promoting harmony within the community.

In these communities, the administration of justice is often carried out by a council of elders or other community members who are respected for their wisdom, knowledge, and experience. These individuals are selected based on their understanding of the community's customs and values and their ability to make fair and just decisions. The council may also include representatives from the victim's family and the offender's family, as well as other members of the community who are affected by the incident.

The process of administering justice in indigenous communities often involves dialogue and consensus-building rather than punishment. The goal is to restore the relationships that have been damaged by the wrongdoing and to find a resolution that benefits everyone involved. This may involve restitution, compensation, or other forms of reparation, as well as efforts to address the root causes of the problem and prevent similar incidents from occurring in the future.

However, the acceptance of the responsibility for the administration of justice in indigenous communities is not without its challenges. The traditional methods of justice often conflict with the legal systems imposed by colonial powers, leading to a lack of recognition and support from the government. Additionally, the use of traditional practices may not always be accepted by younger generations who have been exposed to different ways of thinking and may not fully understand the cultural significance of these practices.

Hence, the responsibility for the administration of justice in indigenous communities is an important aspect of maintaining cultural identity and promoting social harmony. It serves as a reminder that justice is not just about punishing offenders but also about healing relationships and promoting community well-being.

12. The community facilitates the healing process between the broken relationship caused by crime.

In the restorative justice paradigm, the community plays a critical role in facilitating the healing process between the broken relationship caused by crime. Rather than leaving the criminal justice process solely to the legal system, the community takes responsibility for addressing the harm caused by crime and promoting healing.

The community's involvement in the restorative justice process is important for several reasons. First, it helps to rebuild trust between the victim, offender, and the community. When the community comes together to address the harm caused by the crime, it sends a powerful message of solidarity and support to both the victim and offender. This can help to promote a sense of community and foster a sense of accountability for everyone involved.

Second, the community's involvement in restorative justice can help to promote healing and closure for the victim. In traditional criminal justice systems, victims are often left feeling isolated and powerless. However, when the community comes together to support the victim and hold the offender accountable, it can help the victim to regain a sense of control over their life and promote healing.

Finally, the community's involvement in restorative justice can help to reduce recidivism rates. By providing the offender with support and guidance, the community can help to address the underlying issues that may have contributed to their criminal behavior. This can help to reduce the likelihood of future offenses and promote rehabilitation.

Thus, the community's involvement in restorative justice is critical for promoting healing, accountability, and rehabilitation. By working together to address the harm caused by crime, the community can play an important role in building a safer and more just society.

13. Punishment is not restorative if it is done out of revenge or through retribution.

Restorative justice focuses on repairing harm and restoring relationships between victims, offenders, and the community. Punishment, on the other hand, often focuses on retribution and deterrence rather than restoration. Punishment can be a necessary response to criminal behavior, but it is not inherently restorative.

When punishment is done out of revenge or a desire for retribution, it can perpetuate cycles of harm and violence. Instead of addressing the root causes of the behavior and working to repair the harm done, punitive responses may simply escalate the conflict and create new victims. Punishment that is not focused on restoration can also perpetuate societal inequalities and injustices by disproportionately affecting marginalized and oppressed populations.

Restorative justice, on the other hand, offers an alternative to punitive responses by prioritizing the needs of the victim, the offender, and the community. This approach seeks to understand the underlying causes of criminal behavior and to address the harm done through a process of dialogue, accountability, and repair.

Restorative justice can provide healing and closure for victims, as they are given the opportunity to share their experiences and have a say in the resolution of the harm done to them. Offenders are also given the chance to take responsibility for their actions and to make amends for the harm they have caused. The community is involved in the process, and is given the opportunity to address underlying issues and to work towards preventing future harm.

In conclusion, punishment is not restorative if it is done out of revenge or through retribution. Restorative justice offers an alternative approach that focuses on repairing harm, restoring relationships, and preventing future harm.

14. What are some of the questions that can be addressed in a restorative justice paradigm for ministry?

a) What is God's view of justice? a) The concept of justice is central to the character of God as described in the Bible. According to the Bible, God's view of justice is that it is impartial, fair, and righteous. God's justice is not influenced by any human biases or prejudices, and it is based on his unchanging moral standards. God's justice is also described as restorative, meaning that it seeks to repair the damage caused by wrongdoing and restore right relationships.

b) What does He expect of us? b) God expects us to pursue justice and righteousness in all areas of our lives. This includes treating others fairly, advocating for the oppressed and marginalized, and working towards systems and structures that promote justice and equity. The Bible also emphasizes the importance of mercy and forgiveness, even in the context of justice. How should we view the unrighteous acts of the offenders?

c) As Christians, we are called to hate sin but love sinners. This means that we should condemn and resist unrighteous acts, but also seek to offer grace, forgiveness, and the opportunity for redemption to those who have committed them. We should strive to see offenders through God's eyes, recognizing that they too are made in his image and are in need of his love and mercy.

d) Does biblical justice include something other than punishment of wrongs committed against God and man? d) Yes, biblical justice includes more than just punishment for wrongs committed against God and man. It also includes restorative justice, which seeks to repair the harm caused by wrongdoing and restore relationships between the offender and the victim. Restorative justice emphasizes the importance of accountability, but also focuses on healing and reconciliation.

e) How do I minister through a biblical paradigm of justice? e) To minister through a biblical paradigm of justice, it is important to first cultivate a deep understanding of God's character and his view of justice. This can be done through prayer, study of scripture, and engagement with the broader Christian community. From there, it is important to seek out opportunities to advocate for justice and mercy in our communities and to work towards building systems and structures that reflect God's vision of justice. This can involve supporting organizations that are doing this work, volunteering time and resources, and engaging in advocacy and activism. Ultimately, ministering through a biblical paradigm of justice involves a commitment to love, mercy, and restoration, even in the face of great injustice and pain.

Furthermore,

Restorative justice is a framework for addressing harm and promoting healing in relationships, communities, and systems. In a ministry context, restorative justice can be applied to a variety of situations, such as:

1. How can we respond to harm caused within our faith community in a way that promotes accountability, healing, and reconciliation?
2. How can we address the root causes of injustice in our society and work towards systemic change?
3. How can we create a culture of empathy, compassion, and forgiveness within our faith community?
4. How can we support those who have experienced trauma and help them to find healing and wholeness?
5. How can we engage in dialogue with those who hold different beliefs or have been harmed by our community, with a focus on understanding and relationship-building?
6. How can we integrate restorative justice principles into our worship and spiritual practices, such as confession, forgiveness, and reconciliation?
7. How can we work towards repairing harm caused by historical injustices, such as colonization or racism?
8. How can we support individuals who have been impacted by the criminal justice system, including those who have been incarcerated and their families?
9. How can we promote a restorative approach to conflict resolution within our faith community and in our wider society?
10. How can we work collaboratively with other organizations and faith communities to promote restorative justice principles and practices in our communities?

15. What did Job discover about the nature of God's justice?

Apparently, Job discovered that God's justice was more complicated than simply receiving punishment for wrongs he had done and blessings for living a righteous life.

Job is a book in the Hebrew Bible that tells the story of a man named Job who experiences great suffering and loss. Throughout the book, Job struggles to understand why he is suffering and questions the justice of God. In the end, Job has an encounter with God that leads him to a deeper understanding of God's justice.

One of the key things that Job discovers is that God's justice is not always predictable or easily understood. Job had assumed that if he was righteous, he would be rewarded, and if he sinned, he would be punished. However, his suffering seemed to contradict this understanding of justice. Through his conversations with his friends and with God, Job begins to realize that God's justice is more complex than a simple cause-and-effect relationship between behavior and outcome.

Job also discovers that God's justice is rooted in God's wisdom and sovereignty. Job realizes that God's ways are beyond his understanding, and that God is not obligated to explain or justify his actions. Job humbly submits to God's authority, recognizing that God's justice is ultimately trustworthy and good, even if it is not always easy to understand.

Consequently, Job's experience leads him to a deeper appreciation of God's justice, which is not simply about rewarding the righteous and punishing the wicked, but is rooted in God's wisdom, sovereignty, and goodness.

16. Discover within Job 40:8 two questions that God asked Job that suggest he knew little about the justice of God?

a) Wilt thou also disannul my judgment?

b) Wilt thou condemn Me?

In Job 40:8, God speaks to Job and says, "Would you discredit my justice? Would you condemn me to justify yourself?" These two questions suggest that Job had a limited understanding of the justice of God and that he had been trying to justify himself rather than trust in God's wisdom and sovereignty.

The first question, "Would you discredit my justice?", implies that Job may have been questioning the fairness or goodness of God's justice. Job had experienced great suffering and loss, and he may have been struggling to reconcile his understanding of justice with his own experiences. God's question challenges Job to trust in God's justice, even when it is difficult to understand.

The second question, "Would you condemn me to justify yourself?", suggests that Job may have been trying to justify his own righteousness in the face of his suffering. Job had maintained his innocence throughout his trials, and he may have been tempted to criticize God's justice in order to make his own case. God's question challenges Job to trust in God's righteousness and sovereignty, even when it challenges his own sense of justice.

Together, these two questions remind Job that God's justice is not limited by human understanding or perspective. Job is called to trust in God's wisdom and righteousness, even when it challenges his own assumptions and beliefs.

17. How did Job respond after God revealed His concept of justice in chapter 42?

In the book of Job, after Job had endured immense suffering and loss, he questioned God's justice and righteousness. He had argued with his friends and challenged God to explain his situation. God finally responded to Job's challenge by speaking to him directly out of a whirlwind in chapters 38-41, revealing His power, knowledge, and wisdom.

In chapter 42, Job responds to God's revelation by acknowledging his own limited understanding and submitting to God's sovereignty. He says, "I know that you can do all things, and that no purpose of yours can be thwarted... I had heard of you by the hearing of the ear, but now my eye sees you" (Job 42:2,5). Job confesses that he had spoken without understanding and repents in dust and ashes.

God then rebukes Job's friends for their misguided attempts to explain Job's suffering and instructs them to offer burnt offerings and have Job pray for them, indicating that Job's faithfulness and repentance had led to his restoration.

Hence, Job's response to God's concept of justice is one of humility and submission, acknowledging that he did not fully comprehend God's ways and trusting in His sovereignty.

Job did repent and admit that he did not understand or know God's concept of justice.

18. When Job saw the righteousness of God, he also saw the justice of God.

Job's story is one of suffering, loss, and ultimately, redemption. Throughout his trials, Job never lost his faith in God, but he did question the justice of his situation. He demanded an explanation for his suffering, and his friends offered various theories, including that Job must have sinned and brought his misfortune upon himself.

However, in the end, God spoke directly to Job and revealed his ultimate plan and purpose. Job was humbled by the experience and realized that he could not fully comprehend the justice and righteousness of God. He acknowledged that God's ways were beyond his understanding and that he had spoken about things he did not understand.

Therefore, when Job saw the righteousness of God, he also saw the justice of God. He recognized that God's justice was not necessarily based on the human understanding of fairness and punishment. Instead, God's justice was rooted in his ultimate plan and purpose, which was beyond human comprehension.

Job's story demonstrates that justice is not always straightforward, and the human understanding of justice is limited. Ultimately, justice is grounded in the divine plan and purpose, and it is only through faith and trust in God that we can truly understand it.

19. It is important to know that God's attributes are one.

In Christianity, God's attributes are often described as being unified or inseparable. This means that each attribute, such as God's love, mercy, justice, and righteousness, are not separate or distinct qualities, but rather they are interconnected and flow from God's essential nature.

For example, God's justice is not arbitrary or separate from God's love and mercy. Instead, God's justice is grounded in his love and mercy and works in harmony with these attributes. God's justice is not punitive, but restorative and seeks to bring about the healing and redemption of individuals and society.

Similarly, God's righteousness is not a separate attribute from his justice, but rather flows from it. God's righteousness is the standard by which justice is measured and the foundation of his dealings with humanity.

Thus, the unity of God's attributes is a fundamental concept in Christian theology and helps to shape our understanding of God's character and actions in the world.

20. In scripture, Jesus is spoken of both, the justice and righteousness of God.

In scripture, Jesus is referred to as both the justice and righteousness of God because he embodies these attributes in his teachings and actions. Jesus taught about the importance of justice and how it should be carried out with compassion and mercy. He challenged the corrupt authorities of his time and defended the marginalized and oppressed.

Jesus also lived a life of perfect righteousness, obeying God's laws and fulfilling the prophecies of the Old Testament. Through his death and resurrection, Jesus provided a way for humanity to be reconciled with God and receive salvation. This act was both just and righteous, as it fulfilled the requirement of justice for sin while demonstrating God's love and mercy for his creation.

Therefore, when Jesus is referred to as the justice and righteousness of God, it highlights the fact that he embodies these attributes fully and perfectly. It also emphasizes the importance of justice and righteousness in the Christian faith and how they are central to understanding God's character and plan for humanity.

21. When justice came to the nations, it brought the righteousness of God, which reconciles those who receive Jesus Christ as Savior.

The concept of justice and righteousness is a common theme throughout the Bible, both in the Old and New Testaments. The justice of God is often described as a characteristic that is synonymous with righteousness, mercy, and compassion. In the Old Testament, justice was typically administered through the law, and the consequences of disobedience were severe. However, God's ultimate goal was always to restore and reconcile His people to Himself.

In the New Testament, the justice and righteousness of God were fully revealed through Jesus Christ. Jesus came to fulfill the law and to reconcile sinners to God through His death on the cross. The Apostle Paul wrote in Romans 3:21-26, "But now apart from the law the righteousness of God has been made known, to which the Law and the Prophets testify. This righteousness is given through faith in Jesus Christ to all who believe. There is no difference between Jew and Gentile, for all have sinned and fall short of the glory of God, and all are justified freely by his grace through the redemption that came by Christ Jesus. God presented Christ as a sacrifice of atonement, through the shedding of his blood—to be received by faith. He did this to demonstrate his righteousness, because in his forbearance he had left the sins committed beforehand unpunished— he did it to demonstrate his righteousness at the present time, so as to be just and the one who justifies those who have faith in Jesus."

Through faith in Jesus Christ, God's justice and righteousness are revealed in a way that reconciles us to Him. This reconciliation brings about a transformation of our lives, as we are empowered to live in a way that is pleasing to God and brings about justice and righteousness in our relationships and communities. Ultimately, the justice and righteousness of God are inseparable and are fully revealed through Jesus Christ.

22. Discover within 2 Corinthians 5:18 the responsibility of every believer.

2 Corinthians 5:18 states, "All this is from God, who reconciled us to himself through Christ and gave us the ministry of reconciliation." This verse highlights the responsibility of every believer to be involved in the ministry of reconciliation.

The passage emphasizes that it is God who has initiated reconciliation through Jesus Christ. As believers, we have received this gift of reconciliation and are now called to extend it to others. This involves actively participating in the work of bringing people into a restored relationship with God and with one another.

The phrase "ministry of reconciliation" means that believers are called to be ambassadors of Christ, working towards the restoration of relationships and the healing of brokenness. This can take many forms, including sharing the gospel with others, seeking to reconcile broken relationships, working for social justice, and demonstrating love and compassion towards others.

The responsibility of every believer is not just to receive the gift of reconciliation but to actively participate in extending it to others. This requires a commitment to living out our faith in practical ways, both individually and collectively as the body of Christ. It is a call to be agents of change in a broken world, working towards the restoration of all things through the power of the Holy Spirit.

Furthermore, we have been given the ministry of reconciliation. In other words, as ambassadors for Christ, we have the responsibility of bringing others to Christ so they can reconcile with God.

23. Restoration is reflected in the Law that was given in the Old Testament, and the new commandment Jesus gave in the New Testament.

In the Old Testament, the Law included provisions for restitution and restoration for victims of crime. For example, Exodus 22:1 state, "If a man steals an ox or a sheep and slaughters it or sells it, he must pay back five head of cattle for the ox and four sheep for the sheep." This shows that the offender had to not only return the stolen property but also provide additional compensation for the harm caused to the victim.

In the New Testament, Jesus gave a new commandment to his disciples in John 13:34, "A new commandment I give to you, that you love one another: just as I have loved you, you also are to love one another." This commandment emphasizes the importance of love and forgiveness in relationships, and is reflected in the principles of restorative justice which aim to repair harm and restore relationships.

Furthermore, the ultimate act of restoration is seen in the death and resurrection of Jesus Christ. Through his sacrifice, he made it possible for individuals to be restored to a right relationship with God, and to experience healing and reconciliation in their relationships with others. This concept is central to the Christian faith and underlies the principles of restorative justice, which seek to restore broken relationships and promote healing and reconciliation.

24. What purpose did the Law serve? (Galatians 3:24):

Wherefore the law was our schoolmaster to bring us unto Christ, that we might be justified by faith

Galatians 3:24 states, "So the law was our guardian until Christ came that we might be justified by faith." The purpose of the Law was to serve as a guardian or tutor, guiding the Israelites and teaching them about God's standards of righteousness. The Law revealed God's moral and ethical standards and demonstrated humanity's inability to perfectly keep them. It exposed the need for a savior and pointed toward Jesus Christ, who fulfilled the Law and made a way for justification by faith. The Law also served as a temporary measure until the coming of Christ, who established a new covenant and fulfilled the requirements of the Law. Therefore, the Law served to reveal humanity's need for redemption, guide them in righteousness, and ultimately point towards Jesus Christ as the solution to the problem of sin.

A schoolmaster/tutor in ancient Greek culture would accompany the children in his care, instructing and disciplining them when necessary. The law was like a schoolmaster/tutor who, by showing us our sins, was escorting us to Christ.

25. When the Word of God became flesh and lived among us, the consummation of the justice of God in the earth yielded righteousness.

The statement highlights the idea that when Jesus Christ, who is referred to as the "Word of God," came to live among human beings, it marked the ultimate fulfillment of God's justice on earth. In other words, God's justice was made complete and perfect through Jesus Christ, who through his life, death, and resurrection, reconciled humanity to God and made it possible for people to receive forgiveness and salvation.

The justice of God is a fundamental aspect of God's character, which requires that all wrongdoing is punished and righteousness is upheld. The law of God, as revealed in the Old Testament, serves as a standard for righteousness and justice, but it also highlights the impossibility of human beings being able to perfectly keep the law. As a result, humanity became separated from God due to sin and was in need of redemption.

Through Jesus Christ, however, God's justice was satisfied, and the gap between humanity and God was bridged. Christ's death on the cross paid the penalty for sin, and his resurrection defeated death, which is the ultimate consequence of sin. As a result, those who believe in Jesus Christ and follow him can experience the righteousness of God and be reconciled to God.

In summary, the statement implies that the justice of God finds its ultimate fulfillment in the person of Jesus Christ, who through his life, death, and resurrection, reconciled humanity to God and made it possible for people to experience the righteousness of God.

26. The law of "lex talionis" was given to limit the revenges of a people without Christ.

The "lex talionis" is a Latin term that translates to "law of retaliation" or "law of retribution." It is often associated with the Old Testament law of "an eye for an eye, a tooth for a tooth" found in Exodus 21:24, Leviticus 24:20, and Deuteronomy 19:21. This law was given to the ancient Israelites to regulate the concept of justice in their society, particularly in relation to crimes committed against one another.

The law of "lex talionis" sought to limit the revenge of a people without Christ by instituting a proportionate punishment for the harm done. In essence, it prevented individuals from taking excessive vengeance on others and encouraged them to seek justice through legal means. For example, if someone caused harm to another person, they were required to compensate them in a proportionate manner, rather than inflicting greater harm or taking excessive revenge.

However, the "lex talionis" was not perfect, and it had limitations. It did not address the underlying causes of the crimes committed or seek to restore relationships between offenders and victims. It was primarily concerned with ensuring justice was served by punishing the offender.

With the coming of Christ, the concept of justice was transformed from retribution to restoration. Jesus taught the importance of forgiveness, mercy, and love, and He demonstrated these qualities in His own life and ministry. Through His death and resurrection, Jesus provided a way for all people to be reconciled with God and with one another.

In summary, while the "lex talionis" served a purpose in regulating justice in ancient Israel, it was limited in its ability to address the underlying issues and restore relationships. Through Christ, the concept of justice was transformed into one of restoration, emphasizing forgiveness, mercy, and love as the means to bring about reconciliation between individuals and with God.

27. The law of retaliation began to teach that revenge was not part of God's justice, and that punishment did not yield righteousness.

The law of retaliation, also known as "lex talionis," was a principle of justice that was common in many ancient cultures, including the ancient Near East. It was a law that allowed for retaliation in kind, that is, "an eye for an eye" and "a tooth for a tooth." This law was given to limit the revenges of a people without Christ and to ensure that justice was served in a fair and proportionate manner.

However, with the coming of Christ, the law of retaliation began to be seen in a new light. Jesus taught that revenge was not part of God's justice and that punishment did not yield righteousness. Instead, He called for forgiveness and reconciliation, and taught that the greatest commandment was to love God and love our neighbors as ourselves.

The apostle Paul also emphasized the importance of forgiveness and reconciliation in his teachings. In his letter to the Romans, he wrote, "Do not repay anyone evil for evil. Be careful to do what is right in the eyes of everyone. If it is possible, as far as it depends on you, live at peace with everyone" (Romans 12:17-18). Paul also wrote to the Corinthians that "God was reconciling the world to himself in Christ, not counting people's sins against them" (2 Corinthians 5:19).

In light of these teachings, it is clear that the law of retaliation was given to limit revenge in a world without Christ, but that the coming of Christ brought a new way of thinking about justice and righteousness. Forgiveness and reconciliation became the central focus, and the law of retaliation was seen as a limited and imperfect means of achieving justice.

28. Jesus came to fulfill the Law, and to provide a higher standard for those needing restoration.

The concept of restoration has been a part of God's plan since the beginning of time, as seen in the Law given to the Israelites in the Old Testament. However, the people's inability to keep the Law perfectly revealed the need for a higher standard and a means of true restoration. This is where Jesus Christ comes in.

Jesus came not to abolish the Law, but to fulfill it (Matthew 5:17). He provided the perfect example of righteousness and obedience to God's will, serving as the ultimate sacrifice for the forgiveness of sins and offering a path to true restoration. Through faith in Jesus, believers can experience reconciliation with God and the transformation necessary to live a life of righteousness.

Furthermore, Jesus elevated the concept of restoration beyond just physical or material compensation to include emotional and spiritual healing. In the Sermon on the Mount, He taught that those who have been wronged should not seek revenge but rather seek to love and serve their enemies (Matthew 5:43-48). He also emphasized the importance of forgiveness, instructing His followers to forgive others as they have been forgiven by God (Matthew 6:14-15).

In this way, Jesus provided a higher standard of justice and restoration that goes beyond mere legalistic compliance with the Law. He showed that true restoration involves not only the settling of debts and the restoration of relationships but also the healing of emotional and spiritual wounds. Through faith in Him, believers can experience the transformative power of God's love and grace, leading to true restoration and righteousness.

29. The fulfillment of justice was not intended to give offenders what they deserved, but to move them towards restoration through the power of love.

Romans 6:23 describes two inexorable absolutes: 1) spiritual death is the paycheck for every man's sin; and 2) eternal life is a loving free gift God gives undeserving sinners who believe in His Son.

The concept of justice in Christianity is closely related to restoration, which involves the transformation of the offender and the healing of the community affected by the offense. Jesus came to fulfill the law of justice, not by simply punishing offenders, but by providing a higher standard for restoration. The ultimate goal of justice, therefore, is not to give offenders what they deserve, but to restore them through the power of love.

Jesus demonstrated this approach to justice in his teachings and actions. For example, when the Pharisees brought to him a woman caught in adultery and asked if she should be stoned according to the Law of Moses, Jesus did not condemn her, but instead offered forgiveness and restoration (John 8:1-11). He also taught that forgiveness should be offered not just seven times, but seventy-seven times (Matthew 18:21-22).

Furthermore, Jesus' death and resurrection provided the ultimate demonstration of restorative justice. Through his sacrifice, he provided a way for offenders to be reconciled to God and restored to their rightful place in the community. This is exemplified in 2 Corinthians 5:18-19, which states, "All this is from God, who reconciled us to himself through Christ and gave us the ministry of reconciliation: that God was reconciling the world to himself in Christ, not counting people's sins against them."

In summary, the fulfillment of justice in Christianity is not about punishment or revenge, but about restoration through love and forgiveness. This approach requires a shift in focus from the offender to the victim and the community, and a willingness to work towards healing and reconciliation.

30. What is the goal of restorative justice ministry?

Most ministries today do NOT address all the parties that are affected by the crime. They either focus on the offender while neglecting the victim and community or they focus only on the victim. Complete healing and restoration only occur when the injuries to all parties are addressed.

The goal of restorative justice ministry is to promote healing, reconciliation, and restoration for all parties affected by crime or harm. This approach recognizes that crime is not just a violation of law, but a violation of relationships and the community. Therefore, restorative justice ministry seeks to repair the harm caused by crime by bringing together the victim, the offender, and the community to address the needs of all involved.

Restorative justice ministry aims to shift the focus from punishment to restoration, offering a more holistic approach to justice that takes into account the emotional, psychological, and spiritual needs of all parties involved. This involves creating a safe space for open dialogue, empathy, and understanding, and facilitating a process of healing and transformation that leads to greater accountability, responsibility, and meaningful restitution.

The goal of restorative justice ministry is not just to resolve conflicts, but to promote social justice and community well-being. This means addressing the root causes of crime and working towards systemic change that promotes equity, fairness, and respect for all individuals. Restorative justice ministry also seeks to empower individuals and communities to take an active role in shaping the justice system and promoting a more compassionate and restorative approach to justice.

Therefore, the goal of restorative justice ministry is to foster healing, reconciliation, and restoration for all involved, promoting a more just and peaceful society for all.

31. God requires that we love one another, as Jesus loved us, and to love our neighbor as ourselves.

This statement is derived from two key teachings of Jesus. In John 13:34-35, Jesus says, "A new commandment I give to you, that you love one another: just as I have loved you, you also are to love one another. By this all people will know that you are my disciples, if you have love for one another." This commandment to love one another is rooted in Jesus' own love for his disciples, which was selfless, sacrificial, and unconditional.

The second teaching comes from Mark 12:31, where Jesus answers a question about which commandment is the most important. He replies, "The most important is, 'Hear, O Israel: The Lord our God, the Lord is one. And you shall love the Lord your God with all your heart and with all your soul and with all your mind and with all your strength.' The second is this: 'You shall love your neighbor as yourself.' There is no other commandment greater than these."

Together, these teachings call us to love others with the same love that God has shown us, and to love our neighbors as ourselves. This love is not based on merit or worthiness, but is a reflection of the unconditional love that God has for all people. As Christians, we are called to live out this love in our relationships with others, seeking to show kindness, compassion, and forgiveness to all, regardless of their background, beliefs, or actions. Ultimately, the goal of this love is to bring healing, restoration, and reconciliation to broken relationships and a hurting world.

32. Our neighbor is the prisoner who offended, the victim who is brokenhearted, and the community which was blinded by a need for revenge.:

In the Bible, Jesus tells us to love our neighbor as ourselves. This commandment includes all people, even those who have committed crimes and are incarcerated. When we show love and compassion to those who have offended, we are fulfilling this commandment and demonstrating the love of Christ.

The victim of a crime is also our neighbor, and we are called to show them love and support as they heal from the trauma they have experienced. Restorative justice seeks to bring healing to both the offender and the victim, recognizing that both have been affected by the crime in different ways.

Furthermore, when a community is affected by crime, it is important to remember that the members of that community are also our neighbors. Restorative justice principles aim to involve the community in the process of addressing the harm caused by the crime and developing solutions that promote healing and prevention.

Ultimately, restorative justice ministry recognizes that all people are created in the image of God and have inherent dignity and worth. By loving our neighbor, including those who have offended, those who have been victimized, and the wider community, we can work towards a more just and compassionate society.

33. Biblical justice is restoration through righteousness to all who receive Christ.

Paul described this view in Romans 3:22: " ... the righteousness of God, through faith in Jesus Christ, to all and on all who believe."

Biblical justice can be defined as the restoration of what is broken or wrong, to bring about righteousness in all aspects of life. The ultimate source of justice is God, and He has revealed His perfect standard of justice in the Bible. The Bible teaches that justice is an important part of God's character, and that He desires justice for all people. This includes both the victim and the offender.

Restoration is the key to biblical justice. When a wrong has been committed, restoration involves making things right between the offender and the victim, and also between the offender and God. This restoration is made possible through the sacrifice of Jesus Christ, who paid the penalty for our sins and made it possible for us to be reconciled to God.

Restorative justice ministry, therefore, seeks to bring about this restoration through various means such as restitution, reconciliation, and rehabilitation. It seeks to involve all parties affected by the crime, including the offender, the victim, and the community.

The goal of restorative justice ministry is not only to hold offenders accountable for their actions but also to bring about healing and reconciliation for all involved. It aims to address the root causes of crime and to provide opportunities for offenders to take responsibility for their actions, make amends, and move towards a better future.

In summary, biblical justice is about restoring what is broken or wrong to bring about righteousness for all involved, and this is made possible through the sacrifice of Jesus Christ. Restorative justice ministry seeks to bring about this restoration by involving all parties affected by the crime and providing opportunities for healing, reconciliation, and rehabilitation.

34. Which epistle of the Apostle Paul serves as a fine example of restorative justice? Philemon
Paul's letter to Philemon serves as a fine example of restorative justice.

The epistle of Philemon serves as a fine example of restorative justice. In this letter, Paul writes to Philemon, a slave owner, regarding his slave Onesimus who had run away and then come to faith in Christ through Paul's ministry. Paul writes to appeal to Philemon to receive Onesimus back not just as a slave, but as a brother in Christ.

Paul could have simply ordered Philemon to release Onesimus, or could have taken legal action against him for mistreating his slave. Instead, Paul takes a restorative justice approach by appealing to Philemon's Christian values and urging him to do what is right, not just what is legally required.

In his letter, Paul acknowledges that Onesimus had wronged Philemon, and offers to make things right by paying for any damage caused by his escape. He also reminds Philemon that they are brothers in Christ, and that he should receive Onesimus back as he would receive Paul himself.

This approach emphasizes reconciliation and restoration rather than punishment and retribution. It shows how restorative justice can be applied even in situations that involve societal structures of oppression, such as slavery.

35. List the concepts found in the epistle to Philemon that demonstrate the principles of restorative justice.:

a) the concepts of rehabilitation (vs. 10, 16),

b) restoration (vs. 17),

c) and restitution (vs. 18-19).

Until I read this letter to Philemon, I didn't' realize what a talented leader Paul was. I knew he was a great theologian, an incredible author, a successful businessman (tentmaker) and church planter, and a compelling speaker.

But in this letter, we see his leadership skills as he competently addressed the situation. He left the decision completely up to Philemon, and didn't trample all over his rights as the slave's owner. And yet, as we see throughout this letter, Paul arranged things so it would be very difficult for Philemon to say no without losing face among his brothers and sisters in Christ.

The epistle to Philemon demonstrates several principles of restorative justice, including:

1. Forgiveness - Paul encourages Philemon to forgive his runaway slave, Onesimus, who has since become a Christian.

2. Reconciliation - Paul writes to Philemon, asking him to receive Onesimus back as a brother in Christ, rather than as a slave.

3. Restitution - Paul offers to pay any debts or damages owed by Onesimus to Philemon, as a way of making things right between them.

4. Healing - Paul acknowledges the hurt and pain caused by Onesimus' actions, but seeks to bring healing and restoration through forgiveness and reconciliation.
5. Community involvement - Paul asks the church in Colossae to support Philemon and Onesimus in their journey towards reconciliation, showing the importance of community involvement in restorative justice.

Thus, the epistle to Philemon demonstrates how restorative justice principles can be applied in personal relationships, leading to reconciliation and restoration.

36. What crime did the slave, Onesimus, commit against his owner, Philemon? Onesimus stole from his master and ran away.

This very heart-warming letter was written by Paul for the purpose of interceding for the runaway slave who had become a faithful Christian. He not only was pleading for mercy for him from his master, Philemon - he was also reminding Philemon of his duty as a fellow Christian toward this man.

37. What course of action did Paul recommend to Onesimus after he became a Christian?

It was agreed that Onesimus would return to Philemon to make amends, even though under Roman law he could face the death penalty.

In the Epistle to Philemon, Paul recommended that Onesimus should return to his master, Philemon, and reconcile with him. Paul urged Philemon to welcome Onesimus back not as a slave, but as a brother in Christ. He offered to personally pay for any wrong that Onesimus had committed, and asked Philemon to receive him with forgiveness and love. Paul's message was that true restoration and justice can only be achieved through forgiveness and reconciliation, rather than punishment and retribution.

This was a volatile situation. Onesimus was a changed man, but he must have been nervous about going back to Philemon. After all Roman law gave slave owners the right to brand the forehead of runaway slaves, lock them in chains, or simply execute them. Onesimus knew he deserved any one of these punishments because he had not only run away from Philemon, but had stolen from him as well. Anything could happen.

38. The Epistle to Philemon is Paul's plea that Onesimus no longer be viewed as a runaway slave, but rather as a brother beloved.

If a man is a stranger, I might make him my slave. But how can I make my brother be my slave? In this relationship as brothers and not slaves, Paul effectively abolished the sting of the "master-slave" relationship.

In the ancient Roman world, slavery was a common institution and it was not uncommon for slaves to run away from their masters. When Onesimus, a slave of Philemon, ran away and later met Paul, he became a Christian and a changed man. Paul recognized that Onesimus was now a brother in Christ and not just a slave, and as such, he encouraged Philemon to see him in the same light.

In his letter to Philemon, Paul writes in verse 16, "no longer as a slave but more than a slave, a beloved brother, especially to me but how much more to you, both in the flesh and in the Lord." This statement makes it clear that Paul is urging Philemon to see Onesimus as more than just a slave, but as a fellow Christian and beloved brother.

Furthermore, Paul also offered to take responsibility for any debt that Onesimus owed to Philemon, indicating that he was willing to make things right between them and reconcile them as brothers in Christ.

Thence, Paul's message in the Epistle to Philemon is one of reconciliation and restoration, urging Philemon to see Onesimus not as a slave who had wronged him, but as a brother who had been transformed by the power of Christ.

39. While the world pursues power and glory, Christians are to pursue the way of the Cross – the way of forgiveness, restoration and love.

The way of the Cross, as exemplified by Jesus Christ, is a way of sacrificial love and humility. It is a path that goes against the values of the world, which often prioritize power, prestige, and personal gain. Instead of seeking these things, Christians are called to imitate Christ by putting the needs of others before their own and seeking restoration and reconciliation rather than revenge.

Forgiveness is a key aspect of the way of the Cross. Just as Christ forgave those who crucified Him, Christians are called to forgive those who have wronged them. This does not mean that justice should not be sought or that wrongs should be ignored, but rather that forgiveness should be extended even to those who do not deserve it. In this way, forgiveness can lead to restoration and healing, both for the individual who forgives and for the one who is forgiven.

Restoration is also a crucial aspect of the way of the Cross. Rather than seeking revenge or punishment, Christians are called to seek restoration and reconciliation with those who have wronged them. This means working towards repairing relationships and restoring the dignity of those who have been hurt. Restoration requires humility and a willingness to admit fault and seek forgiveness.

Love is the foundation of the way of the Cross. Christ's sacrificial love on the Cross is the ultimate example of love in action, and Christians are called to love others in the same way. This means seeking the good of others, even at personal cost, and putting the needs of others before one's own desires. Love is a transformative force that can bring healing, restoration, and reconciliation.

In summary, the way of the Cross is a path of forgiveness, restoration, and love. It is a way that goes against the values of the world, but leads to true healing and transformation. As Christians, we are called to imitate Christ in all things, including the way we interact with others. By following the way of the Cross, we can be agents of God's love and restoration in the world.

40. No matter what a person has done in the past, God calls them to Himself and offers them the hope of restorative justice.

Paul recognized this fact when he recorded these words in First Timothy 1:15: "Christ Jesus came into the world to save sinners, of whom I am chief." Paul had been a persecutor and murderer of the followers of Christ, but God called him to Himself and offered him the hope of restorative justice.

The message of the gospel is one of hope and redemption. It is a message that God loves us, despite our failures and sins, and desires to restore us to a right relationship with Him. This hope is available to all people, no matter what they have done in the past.

Throughout the Bible, we see examples of individuals who were given a second chance by God. David, for example, committed adultery and murder, but when he repented, God forgave him and restored him to his position as king. The apostle Paul, who persecuted Christians before his conversion, went on to become one of the greatest evangelists in history.

God's desire for restorative justice is seen in His provision of a way for our sins to be forgiven through Jesus Christ. When we repent and turn to Him, He forgives us and begins the process of restoring us to a right relationship with Him. This process may involve discipline and correction, but it is ultimately for our good and His glory.

As Christians, we are called to extend this message of restorative justice to others. We are called to love our neighbors and to seek to restore those who have been broken by sin and injustice. This may involve advocating for the rights of the oppressed, providing support to victims of crime, and working towards reconciliation between offenders and their victims.

In all of our efforts towards restorative justice, we must remember that it is only through the power of God's love and grace that true restoration can take place. We are not called to be judges or to seek revenge, but to extend the same forgiveness and mercy that we have received from God to others.

41. The forgiveness granted by God and by others is what makes restoration possible.

Forgiveness is an essential component of restorative justice because it allows for healing and reconciliation to take place. When someone has wronged another person, the relationship between them is damaged, and forgiveness is necessary for that relationship to be restored. Without forgiveness, the wronged person may hold onto anger, bitterness, and resentment towards the offender, preventing any chance of restoration.

God's forgiveness is offered freely to all who come to Him in repentance, acknowledging their wrongdoing and asking for His forgiveness. This forgiveness is not based on our own merit or worthiness but on God's grace and love for us. Similarly, when someone wrongs us, forgiving them is an act of grace and love, not based on their merit or worthiness, but on our desire to restore the relationship and move forward in love and reconciliation.

In the context of restorative justice, forgiveness allows both the offender and the victim to move towards healing and restoration. The offender can acknowledge their wrongdoing, seek forgiveness, and work towards making amends and rebuilding trust. The victim can choose to forgive and release their anger and bitterness towards the offender, allowing them to move forward in healing and reconciliation. Overall, forgiveness is a crucial aspect of restorative justice as it allows for the possibility of restoration and healing for all parties involved.

CHAPTER 09

RESTORATIVE JUSTICE IN CHRISTIAN COMMUNITIES

Restorative justice is increasingly finding a place within Christian communities as a way to address conflicts and harm while aligning with Christian values and principles. Here's how restorative justice is applied in Christian communities:

1. Biblical Foundations: Restorative justice aligns with many biblical principles of forgiveness, reconciliation, and redemption. Christian communities often draw on these foundations to justify and implement restorative justice practices.

2. Confession and Repentance: Christian communities emphasize the importance of confession and repentance as part of restorative justice processes. Offenders are encouraged to acknowledge their wrongdoing and seek forgiveness.

3. Forgiveness and Reconciliation: The Christian ethos of forgiveness and reconciliation is central to restorative justice. Victims are encouraged to forgive, and offenders are offered a path to redemption through restitution and making amends.

4. Church-Based Mediation: Many Christian communities have established mediation and reconciliation ministries to facilitate restorative justice processes. Trained mediators work with individuals involved in conflicts or harm to find resolution.

5. Accountability: Restorative justice in Christian communities' places importance on holding individuals

accountable for their actions. It recognizes that repentance and forgiveness can be accompanied by accountability.

6. Community Involvement: Christian communities often emphasize the involvement of the broader faith community in the process. This communal approach to justice aligns with restorative justice's emphasis on community support and healing.

7. Practices like Circles: Restorative justice practices like peacemaking circles, where individuals sit in a circle and discuss issues, find resonance in Christian communities as they provide a structured way to address harm, encourage communication, and promote healing.

8. Teaching and Preaching: Clergy and religious leaders incorporate restorative justice principles into their teachings and sermons, encouraging congregants to live out these values in their daily lives.

9. Redemption and Reintegration: Christian communities believe in the potential for redemption and reintegration into the faith community. Restorative justice supports this by offering a path for offenders to reintegrate after making amends.

10. Restorative Approaches to Conflicts: Intra-church disputes or conflicts within Christian communities can be addressed through restorative practices rather than adversarial or punitive methods.

By applying restorative justice within Christian communities, individuals are encouraged to embody the principles of love, forgiveness, and reconciliation. It promotes a sense of community, empathy, and healing, creating a space where individuals can address harm, seek redemption, and strengthen relationships based on Christian values.

1. Although the primary goal of restorative justice ministry in Christian Communities is the regeneration of the offender, other issues concerning their crime and the impact of that behavior need to be addressed.

Most regenerated offenders who come out of prison without having addressed the impact of their criminal behavior will often believe that society owes them something. Crime and the impact of that behavior needs to be addressed in order to eliminate this misconception and because it is vital to the restorative justice process.

Restorative justice is a multifaceted approach to crime that focuses on healing and restoration, rather than solely on punishment. While the regeneration of the offender is a primary goal of restorative justice ministry, it is not the only issue that needs to be addressed.

When a crime is committed, it affects not only the offender but also the victim and the community. Therefore, restorative justice also seeks to address the harm caused by the crime and to make amends for the damage done. This includes addressing issues of accountability and responsibility, repairing harm, and reconciling relationships.

Restorative justice ministry recognizes that offenders must be held accountable for their actions and that they must make amends for the harm they have caused. This can take various forms, such as restitution, community service, or counseling. Additionally, offenders must acknowledge their responsibility for their actions and express remorse for the harm they have caused.

Restorative justice ministry also recognizes the importance of supporting the victim and addressing their needs. This can involve providing emotional support, financial assistance, or other forms of restitution. Victims must also be given a voice in the process, allowing them to express their feelings and concerns and to participate in the restoration process.

Finally, restorative justice ministry recognizes that crimes have a broader impact on the community as a whole. Therefore, the restoration process must involve the community, including community leaders and other stakeholders, in addressing the root causes of crime and working together to promote healing and reconciliation.

In conclusion, while the regeneration of the offender is an important goal of restorative justice ministry, it is only one aspect of a broader process that seeks to address the harm caused by the crime and to promote healing and restoration for all parties involved.

2. When you minister to the needs of the offender, you must not forget that one of their needs is to be healed of the injury of the crime through:

When ministering to the needs of an offender in a restorative justice context, it is important to acknowledge and address the harm that their actions have caused to others. This requires a focus not only on the offender's rehabilitation and restoration, but also on the needs of the victim and the wider community.

The offender may need to make amends for their actions, both through restitution and through actions that seek to repair the harm caused. This may involve making reparations to the victim, such as paying for damages or providing other forms of compensation. It may also involve participating in community service or other activities that benefit those affected by their behavior.

Additionally, the offender may need to address any underlying issues that contributed to their behavior, such as addiction, mental health problems, or a history of trauma. This may involve connecting them with appropriate resources and support, such as counseling, treatment programs, or support groups.

Therefore, a restorative justice approach seeks to address the needs of all parties involved, with a focus on healing and restoration rather than punishment and retribution. By ministering to the needs of the offender holistically, we can work towards building a more just and compassionate society.

3. What marks the beginning of the restorative justice process in the offender's life?

Part of that healing process is to right the wrongs as much as it is in the power of the offender to do so.

The beginning of the restorative justice process in the offender's life is when they take responsibility for their actions and show genuine remorse for the harm they have caused. This may involve admitting guilt, making restitution, and seeking forgiveness from those affected by their actions. It is important for the offender to acknowledge the harm they have caused and to take steps towards making things right. Only then can the process of restoration begin.

4. In a restorative justice paradigm, the offender at some point recognizes the hurt he has caused, and experiences shame for his actions, a shame and sorrow which leads to repentance.

Correct. In 2 Corinthians 7:10, Paul explained that repentance is a result of "godly sorrow", which is very different from human remorse that has no redemptive capability. Human remorse is nothing more than the wounded pride of getting caught in a sin and having one's lust go unfulfilled. This kind of sorrow leads only to guilt, shame, despair, depression, self-pity, hopelessness, and death.

In a restorative justice paradigm, the offender is not only held accountable for their actions but is also allowed to take responsibility for their actions and make amends. This can only happen when the offender recognizes the harm they have caused and experiences genuine remorse for their actions.

This recognition and remorse often come through a process of deep reflection and self-examination. The offender may be encouraged to acknowledge the full extent of the harm they have caused, and to understand how their actions have affected not only their victim, but also their family, their community, and themselves. Through this process, the offender may come to understand the gravity of their actions and the need for accountability.

This recognition and remorse can lead to genuine repentance, which involves not only feeling sorry for one's actions, but also taking concrete steps to make things right. This can include making restitution to the victim, participating in counseling or treatment programs to address underlying issues that led to the offense, and engaging in community service or other activities to make amends for the harm caused.

In short, the beginning of the restorative justice process in the offender's life is marked by a genuine recognition of the harm caused, a deep sense of remorse, and a willingness to take responsibility for one's actions and make things right.

5. Repentance goes far beyond accepting Christ as one's personal Savior; it is a decision to change behavior, attitudes, and beliefs that are not in agreement with the Word of God.

Repentance is a crucial aspect of the Christian faith and a necessary step in the process of restorative justice. It is a decision to turn away from one's old way of life and turn towards God's way of living. It involves a change in behavior, attitudes, and beliefs that are not in agreement with the Word of God.

True repentance is not just about feeling sorry for one's actions; it is a genuine desire to change and make amends for the harm caused. In the context of restorative justice, repentance is the first step towards making things right with the victim and the community. It is a recognition that one's actions have hurt others and a willingness to take responsibility for the harm caused.

Repentance involves confessing one's wrongdoing and seeking forgiveness from God and those who have been hurt. It requires humility, vulnerability, and a willingness to face the consequences of one's actions. It is only through genuine repentance that the offender can begin the process of restoration and reconciliation.

In summary, repentance is a vital part of the restorative justice process. It is a decision to turn away from one's old way of life and turn towards God's way of living. It involves a change in behavior, attitudes, and beliefs that are not in agreement with the Word of God. Repentance is the first step towards making things right with the victim and the community and is necessary for true restoration and reconciliation to take place.

6. The restorative justice paradigm suggests that the offender not only has to be restored through repentance but also must become a restorer through restorer.

It is very common for even regenerated offenders to harbor bitterness, hatred, and resentment toward members of the criminal justice community. They may even view this as a right resulting from the way they were treated while serving time. According to Hebrews 12:15, these types of feelings "cause trouble"; therefore, the offender must learn to forgive.

Restorative justice is a philosophy and approach to justice that focuses on repairing the harm caused by criminal behavior rather than punishing the offender. It seeks to restore relationships between the offender, victim, and community, rather than simply punishing the offender. One of the key principles of restorative justice is the idea that the offender should not only be restored through repentance but also become a restorer through restoration.

Restoration in the context of restorative justice involves repairing the harm caused by the offense. This can involve several steps, including acknowledging the harm done, taking responsibility for the offense, making amends to the victim, and working to prevent similar harm from occurring in the future. Restoration aims to bring about healing and reconciliation between the offender, victim, and community.

The idea that the offender should become a restorer through restoration means that the offender must not only be restored but also play an active role in restoring the harm they caused. This involves taking steps to make amends, such as apologizing to the victim, offering restitution, or engaging in community service. It also involves working to prevent future harm by addressing the underlying causes of the offense and taking steps to avoid similar behavior in the future.

By becoming a restorer through restoration, the offender can demonstrate their commitment to repairing the harm they caused and to making positive changes in their life. This can help to rebuild trust between the offender, victim, and community and can contribute to a sense of justice and healing.

In conclusion, the restorative justice paradigm suggests that the offender not only has to be restored through repentance, but also must become a restorer through restoration. This involves taking responsibility for the harm caused, making amends, and working to prevent future harm. By becoming a restorer, the offender can demonstrate their commitment to repairing the harm and making positive changes in their life, which can contribute to healing and reconciliation.

7. Ministry from a restorative justice paradigm has to address the issues concerning the injury to the victim of the offense(s).

Restorative justice is a philosophy and approach to justice that focuses on repairing harm caused by criminal behavior rather than punishing the offender. It seeks to restore relationships between the offender, victim, and community, rather than simply punishing the offender. One of the key principles of restorative justice is the idea that ministry from this paradigm must address the issues concerning the injury to the victim(s) of the offense(s).

When ministry is approached from a restorative justice paradigm, the needs of the victim(s) are given priority. This involves addressing the injury caused by the offense(s) and working to repair the harm. The goal of restorative justice ministry is to bring about healing and reconciliation between the offender, victim, and community.

To address the issues concerning the injury to the victim(s) of the offense(s), restorative justice ministry may involve several steps. These may include:

1. Acknowledging the harm done: This involves recognizing and acknowledging the impact of the offense(s) on the victim(s). It involves listening to their experiences and feelings, and validating their pain.
2. Offering support and care: Restorative justice ministry must provide care and support to the victim(s). This can include emotional support, practical assistance, and access to resources to help them heal.
3. Facilitating communication: Restorative justice ministry can facilitate communication between the offender and victim(s). This can help the offender to take responsibility for their actions, apologize for the harm caused, and work to make amends.
4. Providing opportunities for the victim(s) to participate in the justice process: Restorative justice ministry can provide opportunities for the victim(s) to participate in the justice process. This can include offering input on the terms of restitution or community service, or participating in a restorative justice conference or circle.
5. Supporting the victim(s) throughout the process: Restorative justice ministry must continue to support the victim(s) throughout the process of healing and reconciliation. This can involve follow-up care, ongoing support, and advocacy for their needs.

In conclusion, ministry from a restorative justice paradigm must address the issues concerning the injury to the victim(s) of the offense(s). This involves prioritizing the needs of the victim(s), acknowledging the harm done, providing support and care, facilitating communication, providing opportunities for the victim(s) to participate in the justice process, and supporting them throughout the process. By addressing the needs of the victim(s), restorative justice ministry can contribute to healing and reconciliation between the offender, victim(s), and community.

8. The victim cannot be the system or the State, which are only abstractions.

In the context of restorative justice, the victim is the person who has been directly harmed or affected by the offense committed by the offender. This can be an individual, a group, or a community. The focus of restorative justice is on repairing the harm caused by the offense and restoring the relationships between the offender, victim(s), and the community.

The system or the state, on the other hand, are abstraction that do not have feelings, emotions, or experiences. While the justice system and the state may have a role in responding to crime and addressing harm, they cannot be the victim(s) of the offense(s). Rather, they are responsible for upholding the law and administering justice in a fair and impartial manner.

It is important to recognize the difference between the victim(s) and the justice system or state in the context of restorative justice. By focusing on the needs of the victim(s), restorative justice seeks to provide a more human-centered approach to justice that prioritizes repairing harm and restoring relationships. This approach recognizes the emotional and psychological impact of crime on individuals and communities, and seeks to address these impacts through a process of healing and reconciliation.

In conclusion, the victim cannot be the system or the state, which are only abstractions. Rather, the focus of restorative justice is on repairing the harm caused to the victim(s) and restoring relationships between the offender, victim(s), and community. By recognizing the difference between the victim(s) and the justice system or state, restorative justice provides a more human-centered approach to justice that seeks to address the emotional and psychological impact of crime.

9. Crime has an impact on human beings, who have feelings and emotions.

Crime has an impact on human beings who have feelings and emotions because it involves the violation of one's physical or psychological integrity, sense of safety, and personal autonomy. When a person becomes a victim of crime, they may experience a range of emotions, including fear, anger, sadness, and anxiety.

For example, if someone is physically assaulted, they may suffer physical injuries and trauma, which can lead to pain, fear, and a loss of sense of control over their own body. Similarly, if someone's property is stolen or damaged, they may feel violated and experience a sense of loss or grief.

In addition to the direct impact on the victim(s), crime can also have an impact on their family, friends, and community. The fear of crime can lead to a loss of trust, a sense of vulnerability, and a decreased quality of life. It can also affect people's sense of safety and well-being, leading to social isolation, anxiety, and depression.

The emotional and psychological impact of crime is often long-lasting and can have a significant impact on a person's quality of life. Restorative justice recognizes the importance of addressing these impacts and seeks to provide a more human-centered approach to justice that focuses on repairing harm and restoring relationships between the offender, victim(s), and community.

In conclusion, crime has an impact on human beings who have feelings and emotions because it involves the violation of one's physical or psychological integrity, sense of safety, and personal autonomy. The emotional and psychological impact of crime can be long-lasting and can have a significant impact on a person's quality of life. Restorative justice seeks to address these impacts by providing a more human-centered approach to justice that focuses on repairing harm and restoring relationships.

10. Whenever there is a direct victim, their pain needs to be addressed so the offender can see how his/her actions affected and damaged the lives of other people.:

"This step is so vital because it teaches the offender how to become a caring member of the community."

The statement that whenever there is a direct victim, their pain needs to be addressed so the offender can see how his/her actions affected and damaged the lives of other people is a central tenet of restorative justice. Restorative justice is an approach to justice that focuses on repairing the harm caused by crime and restoring relationships between the offender, victim(s), and community.

In a restorative justice process, the offender is given an opportunity to take responsibility for their actions, acknowledge the harm they have caused, and make amends to the victim(s) and community. This process requires the offender to confront the impact of their actions on others, including the pain and suffering of the victim(s).

When the pain of the victim(s) is addressed, it can have a powerful impact on the offender. Seeing and understanding the direct impact of their actions on others can help the offender develop empathy and understanding, leading to a greater sense of remorse and accountability for their actions. This, in turn, can lead to a greater likelihood of the offender taking steps to make amends, and less likely to reoffend.

Addressing the pain of the victim(s) is also an important aspect of healing and recovery for the victim(s). By being given a voice and having their pain acknowledged, victims can feel empowered and validated. They may also be more likely to forgive the offender and move forward in their own healing process.

In conclusion, addressing the pain of the victim(s) is a crucial aspect of the restorative justice process. It allows the offender to confront the impact of their actions, develop empathy and understanding, and take responsibility for their behavior. It also empowers and validates the victim(s) and can contribute to their own healing and recovery.

11. Research shows that it is much easier to continue to offend an abstraction than it is to re-offend human beings.

The statement that research shows it is much easier to continue to offend an abstraction than it is to re-offend human beings highlights an important aspect of restorative justice. Restorative justice recognizes that crime is not just a violation of the law, but also a violation of human relationships and social bonds. Therefore, it seeks to address the harm caused by crime by restoring those relationships and bonds.

In traditional criminal justice systems, the focus is on punishing the offender and protecting society from further harm. This often involves treating the offender as an abstract criminal, rather than a human being who has caused harm to others. This approach can lead to a cycle of re-offending, as the offender does not fully understand the harm they have caused and may not be motivated to change their behavior.

Restorative justice, on the other hand, seeks to hold the offender accountable for their actions by making them confront the harm they have caused and take responsibility for it. By engaging with the victim(s) and the community, the offender is able to see the real impact of their actions and to develop empathy and understanding.

Research has shown that this approach is effective in reducing reoffending rates. When offenders are given the opportunity to make amends and to rebuild relationships with their victims and community, they are less likely to reoffend. This is because they have a greater understanding of the harm they have caused and are motivated to change their behavior to prevent future harm.

In conclusion, restorative justice recognizes that crime is not just a violation of the law, but also a violation of human relationships and social bonds. By focusing on repairing harm and restoring relationships, restorative justice is able to address the underlying causes of offending behavior and reduce reoffending rates. This is because it is much easier to continue to offend an abstraction than it is to re-offend human beings, and by making offenders confront the harm they have caused and take responsibility for it, restorative justice creates an environment in which offenders are motivated to change their behavior and make amends for the harm they have caused.

11. Describe a mentor's role with the offender.:

a) is to be a friend,

b) to advise,

c) to help

d) and to model the Christian life for the offender.

Proverbs 27:17 says, "Iron sharpeneth iron; so a man sharpeneth the countenance of his friend." Personal and spiritual growth is a communal affair, as Scripture reminds us in various ways. In the beginning, God did not make just one human being but two (Genesis 1:26–27).

David had Nathan the prophet, a faithful friend who brought him to repentance (2 Samuel 12:1–15). And Jesus appointed not just one overseer; rather, He has chosen for His church to be governed by a body of elders and deacons (Acts 6:1–7). Not just ex-offenders, but we ALL need others in our lives to sharpen us and encourage us in our daily walk.

Those of us who have at least one friend upon whom we can count for loving, constructive criticism are blessed. If we do not have any such people in our lives, we should be looking for them. We should also be asking the Lord to help develop us into people who can offer such criticism to others and to enable us to persist in love toward our friends and others.

In a restorative justice context, a mentor plays an important role in supporting and guiding the offender as they work to repair the harm caused by their actions and take steps to prevent future offending behavior.

The mentor's role is to act as a positive role model for the offender and to provide guidance, support, and encouragement throughout the restorative justice process. This can involve helping the offender to understand the impact of their actions on others, to take responsibility for their behavior, and to develop strategies for making amends and preventing future harm.

In addition, the mentor may provide practical support to the offender, such as helping them to access education or employment opportunities or connecting them with other resources in the community. The mentor may also work with the offender's family and community to help create a supportive environment that encourages positive change.

The mentor's role is not to judge or punish the offender, but rather to support them in the harm caused by their actions and to become a responsible and productive member of the community. The mentor should be non-judgmental, empathetic, and respectful of the offender's feelings and experiences.

Accordingly, the mentor's role with the offender is to help them develop the skills and attitudes necessary to make positive changes in their lives and to prevent future harm. By providing guidance, support, and encouragement, the mentor can help the offender to see the potential for positive change and to take concrete steps towards a more positive future.

12. Which aspect of the criminal justice ministry could easily be listed with the victims of crime?

The offender's family and loved ones should always be listed with the victims of crime because they too suffer from the offender's criminal behavior. Even the sanctions levied against the offender, as a result of their crime, is felt by their family and loved ones.

One aspect of criminal justice ministry that could easily be listed with the victims of crime is the need for healing and restoration. Crime can cause significant harm to victims, including physical, emotional, and psychological trauma. Victims may experience feelings of fear, anxiety, anger, and hopelessness, and may struggle to trust others or feel safe in their communities.

Criminal justice ministry can play an important role in supporting victims in their journey towards healing and restoration. This can involve providing emotional support, counseling, and other resources to help victims cope with the aftermath of the crime. It can also involve advocating for victims' rights and needs within the criminal justice system, such as ensuring that victims are informed about court proceedings and have the opportunity to share their story in court.

In addition, criminal justice ministry can work to promote a restorative justice approach that emphasizes repairing the harm caused by crime and restoring relationships between victims, offenders, and the community. This approach recognizes that crime is not just a violation of the law, but also a violation of human relationships and social bonds, and seeks to address the underlying causes of offending behavior.

By focusing on healing and restoration, criminal justice ministry can help victims to feel heard, supported, and empowered in the aftermath of a crime. It can also help to prevent future harm by addressing the root causes of offending behavior and promoting a more just and peaceful society.

13. Incarceration produces what has been dubbed a prison widow or widower, and the prison orphan.

Incarceration can have significant negative impacts not only on the individual who is incarcerated, but also on their loved ones and family members. The term "prison widow" or "prison widower" is used to describe the partners of incarcerated individuals who may experience a sense of loneliness, isolation, and loss while their loved one is in prison. These individuals may struggle to maintain relationships, raise children, and manage the responsibilities of daily life while their partner is incarcerated.

Similarly, the term "prison orphan" is used to describe children who have one or both parents incarcerated. These children may experience emotional distress, academic challenges, and financial hardship as a result of their parent's incarceration. They may also face stigma and social exclusion due to their parent's status as an incarcerated individual.

The impact of incarceration on family members and loved ones can be profound and long-lasting, and may contribute to cycles of intergenerational poverty, trauma, and social exclusion. As a result, criminal justice systems and ministries should consider the needs and experiences of families and loved ones of incarcerated individuals as they work to address the harms caused by crime and promote a more just and equitable society.

Restorative justice approaches that prioritize healing, restoration, and community engagement may offer a more effective and humane response to crime that recognizes the interconnectedness of individuals and families within communities. By addressing the harms caused by crime in a way that involves and supports all members of the community, including families and loved ones of incarcerated individuals, we can work towards a more just and peaceful society for all.

14. As the offender's family waits on them, they need help spiritually, emotionally and financially.

When a family member is incarcerated, it can have significant emotional, financial, and spiritual impacts on their loved ones. The experience of having a family member in prison can be stressful, traumatic, and isolating, and can leave family members struggling to cope with a range of challenges.

Spiritually, family members may experience a sense of guilt or shame, as well as a sense of disconnection from their faith community. They may struggle to reconcile their love for their incarcerated family member with their own sense of moral values and beliefs.

Emotionally, family members may experience a range of negative emotions such as anxiety, depression, anger, and grief. They may feel a sense of loss, isolation, and shame, as well as a sense of responsibility for their loved one's actions.

Financially, incarceration can impose significant costs on families, including legal fees, travel expenses, and loss of income due to the incarceration of a family member. This can lead to economic hardship, debt, and financial insecurity for the family.

Given these challenges, criminal justice ministries and other support systems can play an important role in helping families of incarcerated individuals. This can include providing emotional and spiritual support, counseling services, and financial assistance. It can also involve working with families to help them stay connected to their incarcerated loved one, such as through visitation programs or letter writing campaigns.

By addressing the spiritual, emotional, and financial needs of families of incarcerated individuals, we can help to mitigate the negative impacts of incarceration and promote healing, restoration, and community engagement. This can also help to prevent future offending behavior and promote a more just and peaceful society for all.

15. There is a great need for marriage seminars that could save literally hundreds of offender marriages, and, as a result, break the generational cycle of crime and brokenness in these families.:

Approximately 90% of all marriages end in divorce when the incarceration period exceeds one year. If the offender can come home to a loving, waiting, Christian family, they have a greater chance of avoiding crime and staying out of prison in the future.

Marriage seminars can be a powerful tool for addressing the needs of families affected by incarceration and breaking the cycle of crime and brokenness that can be passed down from generation to generation. When a family member is incarcerated, it can have significant impacts on their relationships, including their marriage or intimate partner relationships. The stress, trauma, and financial strain associated with incarceration can strain these relationships and lead to divorce or separation.

By providing marriage seminars that address the unique needs of families affected by incarceration, criminal justice ministries and other support systems can help to strengthen relationships, promote healthy communication and conflict resolution skills, and provide a sense of hope and healing to families who may be struggling. These seminars can also help to address the specific challenges faced by families of incarcerated individuals, such as financial strain and emotional distress.

By promoting healthy relationships and strengthening families, marriage seminars can also help to break the cycle of crime and brokenness that can be passed down from generation to generation. Research has shown that children of incarcerated parents are at higher risk for involvement in criminal behavior themselves. By addressing the needs of families affected by incarceration, we can help to prevent future offending behavior and promote a more just and peaceful society for all.

In addition to marriage seminars, criminal justice ministries and other support systems can also provide a range of other services to support families affected by incarceration, such as counseling, financial assistance, and job training. By taking a holistic and restorative approach to criminal justice, we can work towards a more just and equitable society that values the needs and well-being of all members of our communities, including families affected by incarceration.

16. Which aspect of criminal justice ministry is the most difficult?

One thing we can do is to recognize and encourage criminal justice professionals who are positively impacting prisoners by their efforts, and inspiring them to become productive members of our community upon release. Theirs is not an easy job.

Criminal justice ministry can be a challenging and complex field, with many different aspects and challenges to consider. However, one of the most difficult aspects of criminal justice ministry is likely working with offenders who are resistant to change or who are struggling with addiction, mental health issues, or other challenges that make it difficult for them to fully engage in the restorative justice process.

When working with offenders, criminal justice ministries may encounter individuals who are deeply entrenched in their patterns of behavior and who may not be receptive to the idea of taking responsibility for their actions or making amends to their victims. This can be challenging, as it requires a great deal of patience, compassion, and persistence to work with these individuals over time and to help them see the value of the restorative justice process.

In addition, many offenders may be struggling with addiction or mental health issues, which can further complicate their ability to fully engage in the restorative justice process. These individuals may require additional support and resources to address these underlying issues and to fully participate in the restorative justice process.

Wherefore, working with offenders who are resistant to change or who are struggling with addiction or mental health issues requires a great deal of patience, compassion, and perseverance. It can be a difficult and emotionally taxing aspect of criminal justice ministry, but it is also an essential component of promoting healing, restoration, and community engagement. By working with these individuals over time and providing them with the support and resources they need to fully participate in the restorative justice process, we can help to break the cycle of crime and promote a more just and peaceful society for all.

17. The first step in ministering to a criminal justice professional is the building of relationships.

The building of relationships is a crucial first step in ministering to criminal justice professionals for several reasons.

Firstly, criminal justice professionals often work in highly stressful and challenging environments that can take a toll on their mental and emotional well-being. By building relationships with these individuals, criminal justice ministries can provide them with a sense of support, connection, and community that can help to mitigate the effects of this stress and promote greater resilience.

Secondly, building relationships with criminal justice professionals can help to break down barriers and build trust between these individuals and the broader community. Many criminal justice professionals may feel isolated or misunderstood by the communities they serve, and building relationships with them can help to bridge this divide and promote greater understanding and collaboration.

Thirdly, building relationships with criminal justice professionals can help to promote the values of restorative justice and community engagement within the criminal justice system. By demonstrating the importance of building relationships and promoting healing and restoration, criminal justice ministries can help to shift the focus of the criminal justice system away from punitive measures and towards a more restorative and community-centered approach.

Therefore, building relationships with criminal justice professionals is a crucial first step in ministering to these individuals and promoting greater healing and restoration within the criminal justice system. By providing these individuals with a sense of support, connection, and community, criminal justice ministries can help to promote greater well-being and resilience among criminal justice professionals and help to shift the focus of the criminal justice system towards a more restorative and community-centered approach.

18. Establishing a relationship requires much patience because the correctional staff in many ways is a closed community that shuns outsiders.

Establishing relationships with correctional staff can be a challenging and time-consuming process, as these individuals often work in a closed and insular community that can be resistant to outside influence or involvement.

Correctional staff work in a highly stressful and challenging environment, where their safety and the safety of those in their care is a constant concern. This can create a sense of isolation and distrust among correctional staff, who may view outsiders as a potential threat or interference to their work.

To build relationships with correctional staff, it is important to approach them with respect, sensitivity, and an understanding of the challenges they face daily. This may require a significant amount of patience and persistence, as trust and rapport are built slowly over time.

One way to build relationships with correctional staff is to seek out opportunities for collaboration and partnership. This might involve offering to provide training or support to staff members, or working with them to identify areas where restorative justice principles could be integrated into their work.

It is also important to be mindful of the boundaries and limitations of the correctional setting, and to work within the constraints of the system in order to build relationships with staff members. This may require flexibility and a willingness to adapt to the unique needs and culture of the correctional environment.

Thus, building relationships with correctional staff requires patience, persistence, and a deep commitment to promoting restorative justice principles within the criminal justice system. By approaching staff members with respect and sensitivity, and by seeking out opportunities for collaboration and partnership, criminal justice ministries can help to break down barriers and build trust with those working in the correctional system, ultimately promoting greater healing, restoration, and community engagement for all.

19. Because of varying work hours, a church should be willing to schedule special activities and develop programs to include ...: these unique individuals

Because of varying work hours, criminal justice professionals may have difficulty participating in traditional church activities and programs. To include these unique individuals, churches should be willing to schedule special activities and develop programs that are tailored to their specific needs and schedules.

One way to do this is to offer flexible scheduling for worship services and other church activities, such as Bible studies or prayer groups. This might involve offering multiple service times or scheduling events on different days of the week to accommodate the varying work schedules of criminal justice professionals.

In addition to flexible scheduling, churches can also develop specialized programs that are designed specifically for criminal justice professionals. This might include support groups for those who work in the correctional system or specialized training programs that address the unique challenges of this work.

It is also important for churches to be intentional about creating a welcoming and supportive environment for criminal justice professionals. This might involve developing specialized outreach efforts or partnering with organizations that work directly with criminal justice professionals.

Wherefore, churches can play an important role in supporting and ministering to criminal justice professionals by offering flexible scheduling, developing specialized programs, and creating a welcoming and supportive environment. By making an effort to include these unique individuals, churches can help to promote greater healing, restoration, and community engagement within the criminal justice system.

12. To the degree possible, offenders should attempt to reconcile the damages they have caused to those affected by their crime.

Restorative justice emphasizes the importance of offenders taking responsibility for their actions and attempting to make amends for the harm they have caused. One key aspect of this process is the concept of reconciliation, which involves making efforts to repair the harm that has been done to those affected by the crime.

Reconciliation can take many forms, depending on the circumstances of the crime and the needs of the victim(s) and their community. In some cases, it may involve a direct apology or a face-to-face meeting between the offender and the victim, where the offender can express remorse and take steps to make things right.

In other cases, reconciliation may involve the offender making restitution to the victim, such as paying for damages or providing financial support. This can be particularly important in cases where the victim has suffered financial or material losses as a result of the crime.

In addition to making amends to the victim(s), reconciliation can also involve efforts to address the root causes of the offender's behavior and to prevent future offenses. This might include participation in counseling or rehabilitation programs, or making efforts to address the social and environmental factors that contributed to the offender's criminal behavior.

While reconciliation can be a challenging process, it can be an important step towards healing and restoration for both the offender and the victim(s). By taking responsibility for their actions and making efforts to repair the harm they have caused, offenders can demonstrate their commitment to making things right and to contributing to the well-being of their communities.

13. Discover within James 5:16 two prerequisites to healing.:
a) Confess your faults one to another, and pray one for another
b) that ye may be healed

These two prerequisites to healing move both the victim and offender toward restoration. In many cases, lasting friendships are also developed.

James 5:16 states: "Therefore, confess your sins to each other and pray for each other so that you may be healed. The prayer of a righteous person is powerful and effective."
From this verse, we can identify two prerequisites to healing:

1. Confession of sins: James emphasizes the importance of confessing our sins to each other as a prerequisite to healing. Confession involves acknowledging and taking responsibility for our actions, as well as seeking forgiveness from those we have wronged. This act of humility and repentance can be a powerful step towards healing and reconciliation.

2. Prayer for each other: In addition to confession, James also emphasizes the importance of praying for each other as a means of healing. By lifting one another in prayer, we demonstrate our care and concern for each other's well-being, and we invite God's healing power into our lives.

Taken together, these two prerequisites to healing suggest that the process of healing involves both personal responsibility and communal support. We must be willing to confess our sins and seek forgiveness, while also relying on the prayers and support of our fellow believers to help us in our journey towards healing and restoration.

14. An offender also needs to understand how his/her crime has affected the community.

Once the offender understands how their crime has affected the community, they will begin to see how they contribute to its stability. As a result, they will take measures to change.

When an offender commits a crime, the harm caused is not limited to just the victim(s). The wider community can also be affected by the crime, either directly or indirectly. For example, a violent crime may cause fear and anxiety in the community, leading to a sense of insecurity and distrust.

Understanding the impact of the crime on the community is an important aspect of restorative justice. It helps the offender to see the wider consequences of their actions beyond the immediate victim(s), and to take responsibility for their role in causing harm.

By understanding the impact of their crime on the community, the offender can begin to see the need for repairing the harm and making amends. This might involve participating in community service or restitution programs, or taking steps to address the root causes of their behavior, such as addiction or mental health issues.

In addition, by engaging with the community and taking steps towards making amends, the offender can also begin to rebuild trust and restore their relationships with others. This can be an important step towards reintegrating back into society and moving forward in a positive direction.

Finally, understanding the impact of their crime on the community is an important aspect of the offender's journey towards restoration and rehabilitation, and is an important component of the restorative justice process.

15. Every time an offense occurs in a community, the trust level between people decreases and the element of fear increases.

Fearing crime is a common and prevalent issue in modern society. The level or extent of the fear of crime depends on various factors like age, gender, and past experiences.

When an offense occurs in a community, it can have a significant impact on the level of trust between individuals. This is particularly true when the offense is violent or involves a breach of trust, such as theft or fraud. When people feel like they cannot trust those around them, it can lead to a breakdown in community cohesion and a sense of isolation.

In addition to the impact on trust, offenses can also increase the level of fear within a community. This is particularly true for violent crimes or crimes that are perceived as a threat to public safety, such as gang activity or drug trafficking. When people are afraid, they may avoid certain areas or activities, leading to a further breakdown in community cohesion and a sense of isolation.

Both the decrease in trust and the increase in fear can have negative consequences for a community. When people do not trust each other, it can be difficult to build strong relationships or work together to address community issues. When people are afraid, they may be less likely to engage with their community or to participate in activities that promote social cohesion and well-being.

Restorative justice can help to address these issues by promoting healing, reconciliation, and forgiveness. By bringing together victims, offenders, and community members to discuss the impact of the offense and to work towards repairing the harm caused, restorative justice can help to rebuild trust and promote a sense of community. By addressing the root causes of crime and taking steps towards preventing future offenses, restorative justice can also help to reduce fear and increase feelings of safety within the community.

Please note that offenses can have a significant impact on community trust and fear, but restorative justice offers a promising approach for addressing these issues and promoting healing and reconciliation.

16. What are some of the things that people may begin doing, as they become increasingly suspicious of other people? (Answers may vary.):

a) they begin to secure their homes,

b) with extra lights

c) locks,

d) sturdier fences,

e) Others may even go to the extreme of purchasing a fire arm.

As people become increasingly suspicious of others, they may begin to do the following:

1. Avoiding interactions: They may avoid interacting with others, fearing that they may be harmed or betrayed.
2. Checking up on people: They may become obsessive about monitoring other people's actions and whereabouts.
3. Questioning others' motives: They may start to question the motives of others, even those close to them, and suspect that they are up to no good.
4. Secrecy: They may become more secretive themselves, guarding their own actions and thoughts, believing that others might use this information against them.

5. Isolation: They may choose to isolate themselves, withdrawing from social situations and avoiding interactions with others altogether.
6. Guarding their possessions: They may become overly protective of their belongings and property, thinking that someone might steal or damage them.
7. Increased vigilance: They may become more vigilant, always watching out for potential threats or suspicious behavior in others.
8. Paranoia: In severe cases, they may experience paranoia, believing that everyone is out to get them or harm them in some way.

Taken to the extreme, "scelerophobia" is the fear of burglars, bad men, or crime in general. For those with this phobia, many normal things become difficult for the suffering individual. For example, a person might go to great lengths to prevent crime (such as locking one's home or constantly checking and rechecking locks to the extent that it becomes an obsession). Many refuse to step out of their home after dark or travel to lonely places for fear of being attacked or robbed. Their phobia leads to constant fatigue as it causes them to believe that they need to be vigilant all the time.

In a brief testimony, there was a young lady who wanted to be counseled by email. She had not left the house in 30 years. She was afraid of everything and collected disability for her anxiety issues. She keeps roosters, hens, and dogs in the yard for protection. The roosters and hens are there to alert her to someone approaching, in case the dogs fall asleep.

Her first email to me was full of initials for all the diagnoses she had received from doctors over the years. I told her that may be the way the world sees her and what the doctors see in her, but this is NOT the way the Lord sees her. I began to write a series of devotionals for her to begin her day, highlighting what the Lord says she is. She made index cards with the verses and left them all over the house.

However, the email therapy did NOT work. The day she got a letter of inquiry from Social Security about her disability payments, she went into the fetal position in bed for three days, paralyzed by fear. She went back on her meds and decided to discontinue her email counseling. But at the end, she agreed to allow me to convert these personalized devotionals into a course. I deleted personal comments, and she even edited the final product for me. She did an AMAZING job of finding errors or better ways to say the same thing. She excelled because she was in her comfort zone – at home.

17. When offenders are encouraged to address the harm that results from their crime, they can begin to see that their actions are not isolated, and that their families, as well as friends and neighbors, suffer from their crime.

When offenders are encouraged to address the harm that results from their crime, they are given an opportunity to see the impact of their actions on others beyond just themselves. This can be a powerful experience that can help offenders to take responsibility for their behavior and work towards making amends.

One of the key ways in which offenders can begin to see the wider impact of their actions is through restorative justice programs. These programs aim to bring together the offender, the victim, and other affected parties to discuss the harm caused by the crime and work towards repairing it. By hearing from those directly affected by their actions, offenders can start to understand the full extent of the damage they have caused.

In particular, when offenders see how their crime has impacted their families, friends, and neighbors, they can begin to recognize that their actions do not just affect themselves, but have a ripple effect throughout the community. They may see that their loved ones have been hurt by their behavior, and that their relationships with others have been damaged as a result.

This realization can be a powerful motivator for offenders to make changes in their lives and work towards making amends for the harm they have caused. They may become more invested in repairing relationships with those they have hurt, and in taking steps to prevent future harm.

Thus, encouraging offenders to address the harm caused by their crime can be a valuable tool in helping them to take responsibility for their actions and work towards repairing the damage they have caused. By seeing the wider impact of their behavior, offenders can start to recognize the importance of making amends and working towards a better future for themselves and their communities.

18. What happens when the offender focuses on the ills of the prison system, rather than address the harm that resulted from his crime?

The offender is not held accountable for the damage they have caused through their offense.

When an offender focuses solely on the ills of the prison system and neglects to address the harm they caused, it can be a form of denial and avoidance of responsibility. This can be problematic for a few reasons:

1. Failure to take responsibility: By deflecting attention away from their behavior and onto the prison system, offenders may fail to take responsibility for their actions and the harm they have caused. This can hinder the healing process for victims and the community.

2. Lack of accountability: If offenders do not address the harm they caused, they may not be held accountable for their actions. This can lead to a sense of injustice for victims and can undermine the legitimacy of the justice system.

3. Failure to address root causes: By focusing solely on the prison system, offenders may fail to address the root causes of their behavior. Offenders need to understand the underlying factors that contributed to their actions so that they can take steps to address them and prevent future harm.

4. Lack of rehabilitation: If offenders do not take responsibility for their actions and work towards making amends, they may miss out on opportunities for rehabilitation and growth. This can make it more difficult for them to successfully reintegrate into society after their release.

Accordingly, while it is important to acknowledge and address issues within the prison system, it is also important for offenders to take responsibility for their behavior and the harm they have caused. By doing so, they can begin the process of healing and growth, both for themselves and for the community.

They forget that what they have done harmed others, and also avoid feeling accountable for the harm they have caused through their actions.

19. A Christian offender needs to be willing to confront the pain he has caused, and discover a way to rebuild the trust that was destroyed by his actions.

As a Christian, an offender must take responsibility for their actions and be willing to confront the pain they have caused to others. This requires a willingness to face the consequences of their behavior and work towards making amends.

To rebuild trust, the offender must first acknowledge the harm they have caused and express genuine remorse for their actions. This involves taking responsibility for their behavior and recognizing the impact it has had on others. The offender must be willing to listen to the victim and other affected parties, and take their feelings and needs into account.

In addition, the offender must be committed to making things right. This may involve making restitution, participating in restorative justice programs, and taking steps to prevent future harm. The offender may also need to seek counseling or therapy to address any underlying issues that contributed to their behavior.

Ultimately, rebuilding trust is a process that requires patience, persistence, and a genuine desire to change. It may take time for the victim and others to forgive the offender, and it is important for the offender to be respectful of this process and continue to take responsibility for their behavior.

As a Christian, the offender may also seek guidance and support from their faith community. This can provide a source of strength and encouragement as they work towards rebuilding trust and making amends.

20. Ministry, using the restorative justice paradigm, ends in the restoration of both the victim and the offender back into the community.

Restorative justice is a paradigm that seeks to repair harm and restore relationships between those who have been affected by crime. This approach involves bringing together the victim, the offender, and the community to work towards a shared goal of healing and reconciliation.

In a ministry context, the use of the restorative justice paradigm can be particularly powerful. By focusing on restoration and reconciliation, this approach aligns with many Christian values, such as forgiveness, compassion, and love.

In a restorative justice ministry context, the goal is to restore both the victim and the offender back into the community. This involves providing support and resources to both parties as they work towards healing and reconciliation. The victim may receive counseling or other forms of support to help them cope with the trauma they have experienced. The offender may receive counseling or other forms of support to help them address the underlying issues that contributed to their behavior.

In addition, restorative justice ministry may involve community involvement, including support groups, mentoring programs, and other forms of community engagement. By involving the broader community in the restoration process, both the victim and the offender can feel supported and valued.

Ultimately, the goal of restorative justice ministry is to promote healing and reconciliation and to create a sense of community that is based on forgiveness, compassion, and love. Through this approach, both the victim and the offender can be restored into the community and can move forward positively and healthily.

21. The Church, as an accepting community, can help with the issues of restoration, and facilitate reintegration for both the victim and the offender back into the community.

The Church can play a significant role in promoting restoration and facilitating reintegration for both the victim and the offender back into the community. As an accepting and supportive community, the Church can provide a safe and nurturing space for those affected by crime to heal and find support.

For victims of crime, the Church can offer pastoral care, counseling, and other forms of support to help them cope with the trauma they have experienced. The Church can also offer a supportive community where victims can connect with others who have had similar experiences and find comfort and healing.

For offenders, the Church can offer a space for confession, repentance, and redemption. Through pastoral counseling, mentoring, and other forms of support, the Church can help offenders address the underlying issues that contributed to their behavior and find a path toward rehabilitation and restoration.

In addition, the Church can play a role in facilitating the reintegration of both the victim and the offender back into the community. Through community outreach programs, support groups, and other forms of community engagement, the Church can help bridge the gap between those affected by crime and the broader community.

Ultimately, the Church can help to promote healing, reconciliation, and restoration for all those affected by crime. By creating a supportive and accepting community, the Church can provide a space for both the victim and the offender to heal, find redemption, and be welcomed back into the community.

22. What is required of a ministry, in order to be holistic?

a) It must consider both the offender and victim;

b) it attempts to meet the spiritual as well as the physical and emotional needs of those involved;

c) and it addresses the offender in prison, as well as after they are released back to the community.

Putting it in simple terms, you must cover all the bases in order to be holistic.

A holistic ministry is one that addresses the needs of the whole person - body, mind, and spirit. This approach recognizes that people have complex and interconnected needs, and that addressing one area of need can have a positive impact on other areas of their life.

To be holistic, a ministry must take into account the diverse needs of the people it serves. This may involve providing support and resources in a variety of areas, including:

1. Spiritual: A holistic ministry should provide opportunities for people to connect with God and deepen their faith. This may involve offering worship services, Bible studies, or prayer groups.

2. Emotional: A holistic ministry should provide support and resources to help people cope with emotional challenges such as anxiety, depression, or trauma. This may involve offering counseling services, support groups, or other forms of emotional support.

3. Physical: A holistic ministry should provide resources and support to help people maintain physical health and well-

being. This may involve offering health education, exercise classes, or access to medical care.

4. Social: A holistic ministry should provide opportunities for people to connect with others and build relationships. This may involve offering social events, community service projects, or other forms of social support.

5. Financial: A holistic ministry should provide resources and support to help people meet their basic needs and achieve financial stability. This may involve offering job training, financial counseling, or emergency assistance.

By addressing the diverse needs of the people, it serves, a holistic ministry can help to promote healing, growth, and transformation in the lives of those it serves. This approach recognizes the interconnectedness of our physical, emotional, and spiritual needs and provides a framework for supporting the whole person.

CHAPTER 10

CHALLENGES AND CRITIQUES

While applying restorative justice within a biblical framework, such as the principles found in the Book of Romans, offers numerous benefits, it also faces several challenges and critiques. These issues should be considered when implementing such an approach:

1. Theological Differing Interpretations: One challenge lies in the diverse interpretations of biblical teachings across Christian denominations and faith traditions. Restorative justice principles may not align with every theological perspective. Theological debates can arise over the scriptural basis and interpretation of reconciliation and redemption, potentially hindering the widespread acceptance of restorative justice.

2. Institutional Resistance: The criminal justice system, legal structures, and established correctional institutions are often resistant to significant changes. Implementing restorative justice within these systems can face resistance from those who are comfortable with the current punitive approach. It requires a substantial shift in mindset and practice, which may be met with skepticism or opposition.

3. Resource Limitations: Restorative justice processes often demand significant resources, including trained facilitators, counselors, and community support. These resources may not always be readily available, making the application of restorative

justice challenging, particularly in areas with limited access to such support.

4. Victim and Offender Willingness: The success of restorative justice hinges on the willingness of both victims and offenders to engage in the process. Some victims may be hesitant to face their offenders, fearing retraumatization, and some offenders may not be open to taking responsibility for their actions. The lack of participant willingness can pose a substantial hurdle to effective implementation.

5. Societal Skepticism: Restorative justice challenges the conventional understanding of justice, which often centers on punitive measures. It may face skepticism from the broader society, which may question the efficacy of this approach. Overcoming this skepticism and educating the public about the benefits of restorative justice is a persistent challenge.

6. Ensuring Equity: A significant critique of restorative justice lies in its potential to perpetuate systemic inequities. Critics argue that it may not adequately address structural issues like racism or economic disparities. There is a need for rigorous attention to ensuring that restorative justice processes are equitable and accessible to all, regardless of social, economic, or racial backgrounds.

7. Measuring Outcomes: Measuring the effectiveness of restorative justice programs and their long-term impact can be challenging. Traditional justice systems often rely on quantitative measures like recidivism rates, whereas the outcomes of restorative justice are multifaceted and may not be easily quantifiable.

8. Lack of Legal Framework: In some jurisdictions, restorative justice may not have a strong legal framework or legislative support. This can lead to inconsistencies in its application and hinder its acceptance and legitimacy.

Addressing these challenges and critiques requires thoughtful planning, robust education, and a commitment to refining restorative justice practices. While not without its difficulties, applying restorative justice within a biblical framework can foster healing and reconciliation, promoting a more compassionate approach to justice.

In the context of the Book of Romans, applying restorative justice within a biblical framework may face certain challenges and critiques:

1. Theological Interpretation: Different Christian denominations and theological perspectives may interpret the teachings of Romans differently. Restorative justice relies on certain theological principles such as reconciliation and redemption, which might not align with every interpretation of the Bible. Disagreements on the scriptural basis and interpretation of these principles can present challenges when attempting to implement restorative justice universally.

2. Resistance to Change: The traditional view of justice in many societies often revolves around punitive measures. Implementing restorative justice within existing legal and correctional systems may encounter resistance from those accustomed to punitive approaches. The shift in mindset and practice required can be met with skepticism and opposition.

3. Resource Limitations: Restorative justice processes demand resources such as trained facilitators, counselors, and community support. These resources may not always be readily available, making it challenging to implement restorative justice, particularly in regions with limited access to such support.

4. Victim and Offender Willingness: The success of restorative justice depends on the willingness of both victims and offenders to participate in the process. Victims may be hesitant to face their offenders, fearing retraumatization, while some offenders may not be open to taking responsibility for their actions. Lack of participant willingness can be a substantial obstacle to effective implementation.

5. Societal Skepticism: Restorative justice challenges the conventional understanding of justice, which is often centered on punitive measures. It may face skepticism from society at large, with questions about its efficacy compared to punitive justice. Overcoming this skepticism and educating the public about the benefits of restorative justice is a persistent challenge.

6. Ensuring Equity: Critics may argue that restorative justice does not adequately address systemic issues like racism or economic disparities. It's essential to ensure that restorative justice

processes are equitable and accessible to all, regardless of social, economic, or racial backgrounds.

7. Legal Framework: In some jurisdictions, restorative justice may lack a robust legal framework or legislative support. This can lead to inconsistencies in its application and hinder its acceptance and legitimacy within the legal system.

Addressing these challenges and critiques in the context of the Book of Romans would require careful consideration, theological dialogue, and a commitment to educating both the faith community and the broader society about the potential benefits of applying restorative justice within a biblical framework.

Theological differing interpretations are challenges that arise due to the diverse ways in which different Christian denominations and faith traditions interpret biblical teachings. These differences can create challenges when applying restorative justice within a biblical framework. Here's why:

1. Doctrinal Variations: Christian denominations and faith traditions may have distinct doctrines and theological beliefs. For example, while one denomination may emphasize certain aspects of redemption and reconciliation, another may have a different theological emphasis. These variations can lead to differing interpretations of biblical passages, including those relevant to restorative justice.

2. Scriptural Emphasis: Different traditions may place varying degrees of emphasis on different sections of the Bible. This means that passages that are central to one denomination's understanding of restorative justice may not hold the same significance for another. This can result in different interpretations and applications of restorative justice principles.

3. Theological Framework: The theological framework within which a denomination operates can significantly influence their interpretation of biblical principles. For instance, certain traditions may have a strong focus on legal or penal aspects of theology, which could affect their views on justice and reconciliation.

4. Historical Context: The historical context in which a particular denomination or faith tradition was formed can impact its interpretation of biblical passages. Historical events and theological

debates throughout the centuries have contributed to the development of specific theological positions.

5. Denominational Leadership: The leadership and theological positions of a particular denomination or faith tradition can also shape its interpretation of biblical texts. The stance of religious authorities within a tradition can influence how certain principles are applied.

6. Interfaith Dialogue: Interfaith dialogue can reveal theological differences among different religious traditions, including those within Christianity. These differences can impact how restorative justice is understood and practiced in interfaith contexts.

Theological debates that stem from these differing interpretations can be a challenge when attempting to apply restorative justice within a biblical framework. It's essential to engage in respectful dialogue and seek common ground while acknowledging that theological diversity is a fundamental aspect of religious pluralism. This diversity can enrich discussions about how to best apply restorative justice principles within a faith context while respecting a wide range of theological perspectives.

Institutional resistance refers to the reluctance or opposition that can be encountered when attempting to introduce significant changes, such as implementing restorative justice, within established systems like the criminal justice system, legal structures, and correctional institutions. Several factors contribute to this resistance:

1. Current Punitive Approach: The traditional approach within many criminal justice systems is primarily punitive, focusing on punishment and retribution as a response to wrongdoing. Those within the system, including law enforcement, legal professionals, and prison authorities, are accustomed to this approach. Introducing restorative justice, which emphasizes reconciliation, restoration, and healing, represents a fundamental departure from this punitive model. This shift challenges the status quo and can face resistance from individuals comfortable with the current approach.

2. Mindset and Culture: The culture within these institutions often reinforces punitive practices. There is a deeply ingrained mindset that revolves around maintaining law and order

through punitive measures. This culture can be resistant to change, as it may view restorative justice as a departure from established norms.

3. Skepticism and Opposition: Introducing restorative justice requires a substantial shift in mindset and practice. It challenges deeply rooted beliefs about justice and correctional practices. Consequently, individuals within the system may be skeptical about the effectiveness of restorative justice, leading to opposition to its implementation. Concerns about its impact on public safety, legal procedures, and institutional practices can further fuel this skepticism.

4. Resource Allocation: Implementing restorative justice often requires additional resources, such as training for personnel, community support, and facilitators. Institutions may resist these additional resource allocations, especially if they perceive restorative justice as a costly endeavor. The allocation of resources can be a contentious issue when proposing this shift.

5. Lack of Awareness: There may be limited awareness and understanding of restorative justice principles within these institutions. This lack of awareness can result in resistance, as individuals may not fully comprehend the potential benefits of adopting a restorative approach.

Overcoming institutional resistance to restorative justice involves a combination of education, training, and collaboration. Efforts to raise awareness about the effectiveness and advantages of restorative justice, as well as providing training for professionals within the system, can help shift the mindset and culture. Building partnerships and coalitions between proponents of restorative justice and key stakeholders within these institutions is also crucial for fostering change. Additionally, highlighting successful case studies and demonstrating the positive outcomes of restorative justice practices can help mitigate skepticism and opposition.

Resource limitations can pose a significant challenge to the effective implementation of restorative justice for several reasons:

1. Trained Facilitators: Restorative justice processes require skilled and trained facilitators who can guide dialogue between victims and offenders. These facilitators play a crucial role in ensuring that the process is fair, respectful, and focused on healing and reconciliation. Training and maintaining a pool of

qualified facilitators can be resource-intensive, and it may be challenging to find individuals with the necessary expertise in all regions.

2. Counselors and Support Services: Restorative justice often involves addressing the emotional and psychological needs of victims, offenders, and affected parties. Access to counseling and support services is essential to help individuals cope with trauma, express their feelings, and work towards healing. However, providing these services can strain existing mental health and support resources.

3. Community Support: Engaging the community in restorative justice processes is vital. This requires community members who are willing to participate as volunteers, provide support to victims and offenders, and create a safe space for dialogue. Limited community involvement and support can hinder the application of restorative justice, especially in areas with fewer resources or where community engagement is not readily available.

4. Economic Constraints: Restorative justice programs may need financial resources to operate effectively. This includes funding for administrative costs, facilities, and materials necessary for the process. Economic constraints can limit the ability of organizations and institutions to establish and maintain restorative justice programs.

5. Geographic Disparities: Resource limitations may be more pronounced in rural or economically disadvantaged areas, where access to trained facilitators, counselors, and community support may be even scarcer. This can result in unequal access to restorative justice services, which goes against the principle of equitable justice.

6. Time and Administrative Costs: Implementing restorative justice takes time and effort, including administrative costs related to case management and coordination. These administrative tasks may require dedicated personnel and financial resources.

Overcoming resource limitations in the application of restorative justice involves a multi-faceted approach. It includes seeking funding and support from government agencies, private organizations, and community partners. Training and capacity-building programs can help develop a pool of skilled facilitators and support personnel. Additionally, exploring innovative approaches, such as online platforms, can help expand access to restorative justice in areas with limited resources. Collaboration among multiple stakeholders, including government agencies, non-profit organizations, and community groups, is essential to address these resource challenges effectively and ensure that restorative justice is accessible to all who can benefit from it.

Victim and offender willingness is vital in the context of restorative justice for several reasons:

1. Voluntary Participation: Restorative justice is based on voluntary participation. Both victims and offenders must willingly choose to engage in the process. This voluntariness is foundational to the principles of empowerment and self-determination. Forcing individuals to participate in restorative justice processes would contradict these principles and could lead to unproductive or even harmful outcomes.

2. Empowerment: Restorative justice aims to empower victims by giving them a voice and a role in the process. For offenders, it offers an opportunity to take responsibility for their actions and make amends. Willing participation ensures that both parties have agency in the process and are actively involved in shaping its outcome.

3. Healing and Recovery: Victims who are not willing to participate may experience further trauma or distress if forced into restorative processes. Their willingness to engage is crucial for the potential healing and recovery that restorative justice can offer. When victims are ready to confront their offenders and seek resolution, they are more likely to experience positive outcomes.

4. Accountability and Responsibility: Offenders who are unwilling to take responsibility for their actions may not genuinely engage in the process. Willingness on the part of the offender is essential for the success of restorative justice. It signifies a sincere commitment to making amends and addressing the harm caused.

5. Outcome Effectiveness: Restorative justice is most effective when participants are genuinely invested in the process and its outcomes. Willing participants are more likely to engage openly, honestly, and constructively, which can lead to meaningful resolution and reconciliation.

6. Avoiding Re-Traumatization: For victims, particularly in cases of serious harm, the process of facing an offender can be emotionally challenging. Willing participation allows victims to engage at their own pace and when they feel emotionally prepared, minimizing the risk of re-traumatization.

7. Building Trust: The willingness of both victims and offenders to engage in restorative justice can build trust in the process itself. Trust is essential for successful outcomes and for fostering confidence in the broader community in the effectiveness of restorative justice.

To overcome the challenges posed by a lack of participant willingness, practitioners and facilitators must prioritize informed consent and provide support and information to help individuals make the decision that is right for them. Creating a safe and respectful environment that encourages open dialogue and acknowledging the concerns and needs of both victims and offenders are essential steps in ensuring that they willingly participate in restorative justice processes.

Societal skepticism refers to the doubts, reservations, or concerns that the broader society may have regarding a specific concept or approach, in this case, restorative justice. Restorative justice challenges traditional punitive models of justice by emphasizing reconciliation, healing, and community involvement. This shift in focus can lead to skepticism from various segments of society for several reasons:

1. Lack of Familiarity: Restorative justice represents a departure from the familiar punitive model of justice that many people have grown up with. This lack of familiarity can lead to skepticism as individuals may not fully understand the principles and practices of restorative justice.

2. Concerns About Public Safety: Some members of the public may worry that restorative justice places too much emphasis on the needs and rights of offenders, potentially at the expense of public safety. Skepticism can arise from concerns about whether restorative justice adequately addresses public safety issues.

3. Perception of Leniency: Restorative justice is sometimes perceived as being more lenient on offenders compared to traditional punitive measures. This perception can lead to

skepticism, especially among those who believe that offenders should face more severe consequences for their actions.

4. Lack of Trust in Offenders: Some individuals may be skeptical of restorative justice's ability to facilitate genuine change and accountability among offenders. They may question whether offenders are willing to take responsibility for their actions and make amends.

5. Misconceptions and Misinformation: Misconceptions and misinformation about restorative justice can contribute to skepticism. This may include misconceptions about what restorative justice entails and its effectiveness in addressing harm and wrongdoing.

6. Cultural and Value Differences: Different cultural and value systems can influence how restorative justice is perceived. Societal skepticism may be more pronounced in communities or regions where punitive justice is deeply ingrained in the culture.

Overcoming societal skepticism about restorative justice requires proactive efforts to educate the public, dispel myths and misconceptions, and highlight the positive outcomes and benefits of restorative practices. This education can be achieved through public awareness campaigns, community outreach, and the sharing of success stories and case studies that demonstrate the effectiveness of restorative justice in addressing harm, promoting healing, and fostering stronger communities. Additionally, engaging in open and respectful dialogue with skeptics can help address their concerns and provide a more accurate understanding of restorative justice principles and practices.

Ensuring equity in restorative justice is essential for several reasons:

1. Addressing Systemic Inequities: Restorative justice must be mindful of addressing the systemic issues that underlie many forms of harm and wrongdoing. Failing to do so could result in overlooking the root causes of some conflicts, perpetuating inequality, and failing to provide meaningful justice for marginalized communities.

2. Preventing Reinjury: Failing to consider equity in restorative justice processes can risk reinjuring already marginalized individuals or communities. If systemic issues like racism or economic disparities are not addressed, the harm can

continue, and individuals or communities may not experience genuine healing and reconciliation.

3. Community Trust and Buy-In: Equity is crucial for building trust and community buy-in for restorative justice programs. Ensuring that these processes are fair and accessible to all members of the community can help foster confidence in the system and its ability to provide just outcomes.

4. Ethical Imperative: There is an ethical imperative to ensure that restorative justice is applied in a just and equitable manner. Equity is a fundamental principle of justice itself, and it is essential for upholding the values of fairness, dignity, and respect for all individuals.

5. Effectiveness: Equity can enhance the effectiveness of restorative justice. Ensuring that marginalized individuals have equal access to and representation in these processes can result in more meaningful resolutions, better compliance with agreements, and stronger community cohesion.

To ensure equity in restorative justice, it is crucial to:

- Address Structural Inequities: Restorative justice programs should acknowledge and actively work to address structural issues like racism, economic disparities, and discrimination that can contribute to harm and wrongdoing.

- Community Engagement: Engage with the affected community and involve them in the design and implementation of restorative justice programs. This helps ensure that the processes are culturally sensitive and relevant.

- Cultural Competency: Provide training to facilitators and practitioners in cultural competency and sensitivity to address the diverse needs of participants.

- Accessible Support: Ensure that individuals, particularly those from marginalized backgrounds, have access to support services to address any emotional, psychological, or material needs they may have.

- Evaluation and Monitoring: Continuously evaluate and monitor the equity of restorative justice programs to identify any disparities and make adjustments as needed.

By prioritizing equity in restorative justice, it becomes a more powerful tool for addressing harm, promoting healing, and fostering stronger, more inclusive communities.

Measuring outcomes in restorative justice is essential for several reasons:

1. Accountability and Transparency: Measuring outcomes ensures that restorative justice programs are held accountable for their effectiveness. This transparency is crucial for maintaining public trust and support.

2. Continuous Improvement: Evaluation and measurement allow for ongoing improvement of restorative justice practices. By understanding what works and what doesn't, practitioners can refine their methods and enhance the quality of services.

3. Evidence-Based Practices: Measuring outcomes provides the opportunity to identify evidence-based practices that have the most positive impact on participants and communities. This can help in refining program models and implementing practices that have proven to be effective.

4. Participant Satisfaction: Understanding participant satisfaction and the perception of fairness is vital. High levels of participant satisfaction often correlate with successful outcomes, as they indicate that individuals feel their needs and concerns have been adequately addressed.

5. Restitution and Repair: Measuring outcomes helps assess the success of restitution and repair efforts. Evaluating whether offenders have made genuine efforts to make amends for their actions and whether victims have experienced healing and resolution is essential.

6. Community Impact: Restorative justice can have broader community impacts beyond individual cases. Measuring these impacts can help demonstrate the value of restorative justice in building stronger, more cohesive communities.

7. Resource Allocation: Resources are often limited, and measuring outcomes helps in making informed decisions about resource allocation. It ensures that resources are directed toward practices and programs that yield the best results.

8. Policy and Advocacy: Outcomes data can be valuable in advocating for restorative justice at a policy level. It provides

evidence of the effectiveness of restorative practices and can be used to advocate for broader implementation and support.

To effectively measure outcomes in restorative justice, it is important to develop appropriate evaluation frameworks and methods. These may include:

- Qualitative and Quantitative Data: A combination of both qualitative and quantitative data can provide a comprehensive view of outcomes. This may include surveys, interviews, and statistical analysis.

- Longitudinal Studies: Tracking the long-term impact of restorative justice on participants and communities is essential. This can help determine whether the benefits are sustained over time.

- Feedback and Participant Surveys: Gathering feedback from victims, offenders, and affected parties about their experiences and perceptions of the process.

- Comparative Analysis: Comparing the outcomes of restorative justice cases with those processed through traditional justice systems can provide insights into the effectiveness of restorative practices.

- Cultural Sensitivity: Ensuring that measurement tools are culturally sensitive and relevant to diverse communities is crucial for accurately capturing outcomes.

Overall, measuring outcomes in restorative justice is important for demonstrating its effectiveness, improving practices, and advocating for its continued growth as a valuable approach to addressing harm and promoting healing.

The lack of a legal framework for restorative practices can present several challenges:

1. Inconsistent Application: Without a clear legal framework, the application of restorative justice may be inconsistent. Different practitioners or jurisdictions may interpret and implement restorative practices in various ways, leading to inequities in access and outcomes.

2. Legitimacy and Trust: A well-established legal framework can enhance the legitimacy and trust in restorative justice processes. It provides a clear mandate for the use of restorative practices, making them more acceptable to the public, victims, and offenders.

3. Standardization: A legal framework can standardize restorative justice practices, ensuring that they meet specific criteria and adhere to best practices. This consistency is essential for the effectiveness and reliability of restorative processes.

4. Procedural Safeguards: Legal frameworks often include procedural safeguards that protect the rights and interests of all parties involved. Without these safeguards, there may be concerns about due process and fairness.

5. Accountability: A legal framework provides a mechanism for holding practitioners and facilitators accountable for their actions. It sets out the expectations and responsibilities of those involved in restorative justice processes.

6. Enforceability: Legal support can make the outcomes of restorative justice processes more enforceable. Agreements reached through restorative practices may have legal weight, providing added incentives for compliance.

7. Public Funding: Legal recognition can facilitate the allocation of public funds to support restorative justice programs. This financial support is crucial for their sustainability and growth.

8. Victim and Offender Confidence: Victims and offenders may have greater confidence in the process when it operates within a legal framework. They may be more willing to participate if they know that their rights and interests are protected by law.

9. Consistent Ethical Standards: Legal frameworks often include ethical standards that practitioners must adhere to. These standards help ensure that restorative justice processes are conducted ethically and responsibly.

To address the lack of a legal framework for restorative practices, efforts can be made to advocate for legislative support and the development of legal guidelines that provide a clear and consistent framework for the application of restorative justice. This may involve working with lawmakers, legal experts, and community stakeholders to create and implement legislation that supports the principles and practices of restorative justice while ensuring due process and fairness. Such efforts can enhance the effectiveness, legitimacy, and acceptance of restorative practices within the legal system.

CHAPTER 11

OVERCOMING THE OBSTACLES

Overcoming the obstacles and challenges associated with restorative justice requires thoughtful strategies and ongoing efforts. Here are ways to address these challenges and make restorative justice more effective and widely applicable:

1. Education and Training: Provide comprehensive education and training for all stakeholders, including judges, lawyers, law enforcement, community members, and participants in restorative justice processes. This ensures a clear understanding of the principles, practices, and potential benefits of restorative justice.

2. Standardization: Develop and promote standardized practices and guidelines for restorative justice processes. This can help ensure consistency and fairness in how cases are handled.

3. Legal Protections: Maintain strong legal protections within restorative justice processes to safeguard the rights of both victims and offenders. Ensure that participation is voluntary and informed.

4. Victim Support Services: Enhance support services for victims to address concerns about re-victimization and retaliation. Ensure that victims have access to information, counseling, and legal advocacy.

5. Community Engagement: Foster community engagement and involvement in restorative justice. This can help

address disparities in access and create a stronger sense of community responsibility.

6. Evaluation and Research: Invest in rigorous research and evaluation of restorative justice programs to assess their effectiveness, identify areas for improvement, and build evidence of their impact.

7. Restorative Justice Legislation: Encourage the development and implementation of restorative justice legislation that outlines its role within the criminal justice system and ensures proper support and funding.

8. Collaboration: Promote collaboration between traditional justice systems and restorative justice programs. This can help address resistance and ensure that restorative justice is integrated effectively into existing systems.

9. Cultural Sensitivity: Adapt restorative justice practices to respect and incorporate the cultural values and norms of diverse communities, ensuring that the approach is sensitive to local contexts.

10. Resources and Funding: Advocate for adequate resources and funding for restorative justice programs to ensure their sustainability and capacity to operate effectively.

11. Public Awareness: Increase public awareness and understanding of restorative justice through public campaigns, educational initiatives, and outreach efforts.

12. Conflict Prevention: Expand the use of restorative justice in conflict prevention, education, and other areas beyond the criminal justice system, where it can foster a culture of dialogue and understanding.

By addressing these obstacles and implementing these strategies, societies can make restorative justice a more viable and effective approach to addressing harm and promoting healing and reconciliation. Restorative justice has the potential to create a more just and compassionate justice system, but it requires ongoing dedication and effort to overcome the challenges it faces.

Contemporary Relevance:

Restorative justice plays a crucial role in the ongoing efforts for criminal justice reform. The contemporary criminal justice system faces a range of challenges, and restorative justice principles, inspired by the teachings of Romans, offer valuable alternatives and solutions to these issues:

1. Over-Incarceration: Restorative justice promotes a more balanced and proportional response to offenses. Instead of resorting to lengthy prison sentences for non-violent and low-level offenses, restorative justice offers a way to address harm and wrongdoing without the need for incarceration. This approach can help alleviate the problem of over-incarceration, which has strained prison systems and disproportionately affected certain communities.

2. Racial Disparities: Racial disparities in the criminal justice system are a deeply rooted problem. Restorative justice principles prioritize fairness, equity, and addressing the root causes of crime. By focusing on understanding and repairing harm, restorative justice can help reduce racial disparities by addressing the underlying issues that lead to criminal behavior, rather than perpetuating systemic bias.

3. Recidivism: One of the central challenges in criminal justice is the high rate of recidivism, where individuals released from prison often reoffend. Restorative justice places a strong emphasis on accountability and addressing the underlying causes of criminal behavior. By involving offenders in the process of repairing harm and taking responsibility for their actions, restorative justice can contribute to reducing recidivism and promoting rehabilitation.

4. Healing and Reintegration: Traditional punitive justice systems often neglect the healing and reintegration of offenders into society. Restorative justice offers a holistic approach that recognizes the importance of addressing the harm caused to victims, helping offenders take responsibility for their actions, and facilitating their successful reintegration into the community. This approach not only benefits individuals but also contributes to safer and more cohesive communities.

5. Community Engagement: Restorative justice actively involves the community in the resolution of conflicts and the reintegration of offenders. This community engagement fosters a sense of ownership and responsibility for addressing crime and its consequences. It encourages collective efforts to create a more just and compassionate society.

In essence, restorative justice provides a promising avenue for addressing the pressing issues within the criminal justice system. It shifts the focus from punitive measures to healing, accountability, and reintegration, aligning with the principles of fairness, compassion, and reconciliation inspired by the teachings of Romans. While it may not replace traditional criminal justice entirely, it offers a valuable and transformative complement that contributes to criminal justice reform efforts and paves the way for a more just and equitable system.

Community and social healing refer to the process of mending and revitalizing the relationships, trust, and cohesion within a community that may have been strained or damaged by conflicts, divisions, or various forms of harm. In today's interconnected world, communities often grapple with a range of challenges, including:

1. Conflicts: Communities may experience conflicts and disputes among individuals, groups, or institutions. These conflicts can lead to division, mistrust, and a breakdown of social bonds.

2. Prejudice and Discrimination: Prejudice and discrimination, whether based on race, ethnicity, religion, gender, or other factors, can lead to social divisions and exclusion. Addressing these issues is essential for building inclusive and equitable communities.

3. Social Divisions: Social divisions can arise from various factors, including economic disparities, political differences, and cultural diversity. These divisions can lead to fragmentation and hinder the well-being of the community as a whole.

In the context of community and social healing, the principles of reconciliation and restoration from Romans can play a pivotal role:

1. Reconciliation: Reconciliation involves bringing together individuals or groups who have been in conflict, helping them understand each other's perspectives, and finding common ground. Romans emphasizes the importance of reconciliation with God and among people, offering a model for addressing conflicts within communities.

2. Restoration: Restoration entails the repair and revitalization of relationships and trust within a community. Romans highlights the value of restoration in the context of personal

transformation and healing, which can extend to the broader community.

3. Healing: Healing addresses the emotional, psychological, and social wounds caused by conflicts, divisions, and harm. The principles from Romans underscore the significance of healing and renewal, both at the individual and community levels.

4. Mending Social Rifts: The teachings of Romans can inform community-based initiatives that aim to mend social rifts. By emphasizing values of forgiveness, empathy, and understanding, these initiatives can create a sense of unity, shared purpose, and social cohesion within the community.

Community and social healing are vital for fostering resilient and harmonious communities. By drawing inspiration from the principles of reconciliation and restoration found in Romans, communities can work towards resolving conflicts, addressing prejudice, and bridging social divisions, ultimately building more inclusive and compassionate societies where individuals and groups coexist in harmony.

Conflict resolution and peacebuilding are essential processes aimed at resolving conflicts and promoting peace, both at local and global levels. In an increasingly interconnected world, various conflicts, whether they are local disputes or international tensions, demand effective approaches to de-escalate and address these issues. Restorative justice, inspired by the principles of Romans, offers a valuable framework for these processes by emphasizing dialogue, understanding, and reconciliation:

1. Conflict Resolution: Restorative justice, rooted in principles of accountability and reconciliation, provides a structured approach to addressing conflicts. It encourages all parties involved to engage in dialogue, understand the root causes of the conflict, and work together to find mutually agreeable solutions. This process can be applied to interpersonal disputes, community conflicts, and even larger-scale conflicts, helping to prevent escalation and fostering resolution.

2. Dialogue and Understanding: Central to restorative justice is the concept of open and meaningful dialogue. This dialogue creates an environment where all parties have the

opportunity to express their perspectives and concerns. Through this process, individuals can develop a deeper understanding of the motivations and needs of others involved in the conflict. Romans' teachings on reconciliation and forgiveness align with the aim of promoting empathy and understanding, crucial elements in any conflict resolution process.

3. Reconciliation: Restorative justice places a strong emphasis on reconciliation, which is the process of repairing and restoring relationships that may have been damaged by the conflict. Romans highlights the importance of reconciling with one another, emphasizing forgiveness and healing. This concept is integral to peacebuilding efforts, as it fosters the re-establishment of trust and cooperation among parties in conflict.

4. Conflict Prevention: While often applied after a conflict has occurred, restorative justice principles can also contribute to conflict prevention. By addressing the underlying causes of conflicts and promoting understanding, individuals and communities can work proactively to reduce tensions and prevent conflicts from escalating.

5. Peacebuilding: Peacebuilding is a long-term process that aims to establish and maintain peace in the aftermath of conflicts. Restorative justice, inspired by Romans, aligns with this goal by focusing on repairing harm, promoting accountability, and fostering positive relationships. It contributes to sustainable peace by addressing the root causes of conflict.

6. International Diplomacy: Restorative justice principles can be applied at international levels through diplomacy and peace negotiations. The principles of accountability, dialogue, and reconciliation offer valuable tools for resolving international conflicts, bridging divides, and promoting lasting peace.

In summary, restorative justice, inspired by the teachings of Romans, provides a framework for conflict resolution and peacebuilding that emphasizes dialogue, understanding, and reconciliation. This approach is valuable not only in addressing conflicts but also in preventing them and contributing to lasting peace within communities and on a global scale.

Truth and reconciliation are integral components of transitional justice in post-conflict societies. Restorative justice principles, rooted in accountability and reconciliation, align closely with the goals of truth and reconciliation commissions. Here's how they intersect:

1. Uncovering Past Wrongs: Truth and reconciliation commissions aim to uncover and document past wrongs, including human rights abuses and crimes committed during conflicts or oppressive regimes. These commissions create a platform for victims and perpetrators to share their experiences and for society to confront its history. Restorative justice principles emphasize acknowledging wrongdoing and the need for truth as a foundation for accountability.

2. Accountability: Restorative justice underscores the importance of holding individuals accountable for their actions. Truth and reconciliation commissions serve a similar purpose by identifying those responsible for human rights violations and ensuring they face appropriate consequences, whether through legal proceedings or alternative forms of accountability. Restorative justice processes within these commissions can include acknowledgment of wrongdoing and sincere expressions of remorse.

3. Victim-Centered Approaches: Restorative justice places victims at the center of the process, ensuring their voices are heard and their needs are addressed. Truth and reconciliation commissions similarly prioritize the experiences and needs of victims, providing a space for them to share their stories and seek acknowledgment and reparations.

4. Healing and Reconciliation: Restorative justice seeks to promote healing and reconciliation, not only between individuals but within communities and society at large. Truth and reconciliation commissions aim to facilitate national healing by acknowledging past wrongs, fostering understanding, and promoting reconciliation. Both approaches recognize the significance of addressing the emotional and psychological wounds left by conflicts.

5. Preventing Recurrence: Both restorative justice and truth and reconciliation commissions aim to prevent the recurrence of violence and injustice. They do so by addressing the root causes of conflict, exposing the consequences of past wrongdoing, and establishing a framework for building a just and peaceful society.

6. Public Acknowledgment: Restorative justice emphasizes the public acknowledgment of wrongdoing, and truth and reconciliation commissions provide a forum for this acknowledgment on a national scale. This acknowledgment is critical for both individual and societal healing and for breaking the cycle of denial and impunity.

In summary, truth and reconciliation commissions and restorative justice principles share a common objective in addressing the legacy of violence and injustice in post-conflict societies. They aim to uncover past wrongs, foster accountability, promote healing, and prevent the recurrence of conflict. The principles of acknowledgment, accountability, and reconciliation are central to both approaches, making them complementary in transitional justice processes.

Restorative practices in schools, while highly beneficial, are not as common as they should be for several reasons. These practices, inspired by principles found in Romans, can play a significant role in addressing bullying and school violence, as well as in creating a safe and inclusive learning environment. Here are some factors contributing to their limited implementation:

1. Lack of Awareness: Many educators and school administrators may not be fully aware of restorative practices and their potential benefits. Awareness and education are crucial to encouraging the adoption of these practices in schools.

2. Traditional Disciplinary Approaches: The traditional punitive approach to discipline, such as suspensions and expulsions, has been the norm in many schools. Transitioning to restorative practices requires a shift in mindset and a willingness to explore alternative methods of addressing behavioral issues.

3. Resistance to Change: Resistance to change is a common barrier in many institutions, including schools. Implementing restorative practices may face opposition from those who are comfortable with the status quo or are hesitant to try new approaches.

4. Training and Resources: Effective implementation of restorative practices requires proper training and resources for educators and school staff. Many schools may lack the resources and funding needed to provide this training.

5. Measuring Outcomes: Some school systems focus on quantifiable outcomes, such as standardized test scores, and may be hesitant to invest in restorative practices that have less easily measurable outcomes, even though the long-term benefits are significant.

6. Complexity of Implementation: Restorative practices involve complex interpersonal dynamics and require a deep understanding of the principle involved. This complexity can deter some schools from adopting these practices.

7. Time and Commitment: Restorative practices demand time and commitment from both educators and students. Some may be concerned about the time investment needed, as well as whether students will be receptive to the process.

Despite these challenges, restorative practices hold great promise in addressing bullying and school violence. These practices encourage dialogue, empathy, and accountability, creating an environment where students feel a sense of belonging and are more likely to address and resolve conflicts in a constructive way. By promoting the principles of Romans – acknowledgment, responsibility, and reconciliation – restorative practices have the potential to create safer and more inclusive learning environments in schools, making them a valuable investment in the well-being of students and the overall school community.

Victims of crime indeed require comprehensive support to navigate the physical, emotional, and psychological impact of their experiences. Modern victim support services can greatly benefit from integrating restorative justice principles to empower victims, address their needs, and facilitate their healing journey. Here's how restorative justice can enhance victim support:

1. Empowerment: Restorative justice principles emphasize the empowerment of victims, giving them a voice and a role in the process. Victim support services can integrate these principles by providing victims with opportunities to express their feelings, needs, and preferences. Empowering victims in this way helps them regain a sense of control over their lives and their recovery.

2. Acknowledgment and Validation: Restorative justice encourages the acknowledgment of the harm done to victims. Support services can use this principle to validate victims'

experiences and provide a safe space for them to share their stories. This acknowledgment can be a crucial step in the healing process.

3. Individualized Support: Victim support services can adopt an individualized approach to meet each victim's unique needs. Restorative justice principles promote tailoring the response to the specific circumstances of each case, which aligns with providing personalized support to victims.

4. Healing-Centered Approaches: Restorative justice focuses on healing and reconciliation, not only for offenders but also for victims. Victim support services can incorporate these healing-centered approaches by offering counseling, therapy, and resources that promote emotional and psychological recovery.

5. Restitution and Compensation: Restorative justice principles include the concept of restitution and making amends. Victim support services can help victims access compensation, financial support, or restitution when applicable, ensuring they receive fair and just reparations for their losses.

6. Restorative Justice Programs: Some victim support services are involved in restorative justice programs, where victims have the option to participate in processes that involve dialogue with offenders. These programs allow victims to ask questions, seek answers, and find closure, contributing to their emotional recovery.

7. Education and Awareness: Victim support services can educate victims about restorative justice principles and processes, allowing them to make informed decisions about their involvement in legal proceedings and restorative justice practices.

8. Long-Term Support: Restorative justice principles recognize that the impact of harm can be long-lasting. Victim support services should also provide long-term support, as needed, to help victims as they continue on their healing journey.

Incorporating restorative justice principles into victim support services can significantly enhance the quality of care and assistance provided to victims. By empowering victims, acknowledging their experiences, and promoting healing, these services can better address the complex and multifaceted needs of victims of crime, ultimately contributing to their recovery and well-being.

The global relevance of the teachings of Romans on restorative justice is evident in their adaptability to diverse regions and cultures. Here are examples from various parts of the world where these principles have been embraced to address local and global challenges:

1. South Africa: The Truth and Reconciliation Commission in South Africa, chaired by Archbishop Desmond Tutu, employed restorative justice principles to address the legacy of apartheid. It allowed victims and perpetrators to come forward, acknowledge wrongdoings, and work towards reconciliation. This approach served as a model for post-conflict societies worldwide.

2. Canada: Canada's Indigenous communities have been applying restorative justice principles in their justice systems. These principles are incorporated into the sentencing of offenders, emphasizing community involvement and the restoration of harmony.

3. Scandinavian Countries: Countries like Norway and Sweden have implemented restorative justice practices in their criminal justice systems. They focus on rehabilitation and reintegration rather than punitive measures, resulting in lower recidivism rates and safer communities.

4. Middle East: Organizations like the Sulha Peace Project in the Middle East use restorative justice principles to promote dialogue and reconciliation in conflict-ridden areas. They facilitate encounters between people of different backgrounds and encourage communication to build bridges.

5. Australia: Restorative justice practices are widely used in Australian schools to address issues like bullying and student conflicts. These practices create a more inclusive and respectful learning environment.

6. Restorative Circles in Brazil: Favelas in Brazil have seen the implementation of restorative circles, a community-based approach to resolving conflicts and promoting social cohesion. These circles have helped reduce violence and improve community relations.

7. The Balkans: The Balkans region, which experienced violent conflicts in the 1990s, has seen initiatives that draw from restorative justice principles to promote reconciliation and healing among different ethnic groups.

8. United States: Restorative justice programs have been introduced in various U.S. states, particularly within the juvenile justice system. These programs aim to divert young offenders from the traditional justice system and provide opportunities for rehabilitation.

9. International Tribunals: International criminal tribunals, such as the International Criminal Court (ICC), draw on restorative justice principles when determining sentences for individuals found guilty of war crimes, crimes against humanity, and genocide.

10. Community-Based Initiatives: Grassroots community organizations worldwide have adopted restorative justice practices to address local disputes, build trust, and promote reconciliation.

The global adoption of restorative justice principles, inspired by the teachings of Romans, reflects their adaptability and effectiveness in addressing a wide range of challenges, from post-conflict reconciliation to school bullying. These principles provide a framework for dialogue, acknowledgment, accountability, healing, and the promotion of a just and inclusive society, making them relevant and applicable on a global scale.

Interfaith and interdisciplinary dialogues are indeed crucial when it comes to leveraging the teachings of Romans on restorative justice. Here's why these dialogues are important:

1. Diversity of Perspectives: Interfaith dialogues bring together representatives from different faith traditions, fostering a rich exchange of perspectives on restorative justice. This diversity helps in creating a more comprehensive and inclusive understanding of how these principles can be applied.

2. Shared Values: Many faith traditions share common values related to justice, forgiveness, and reconciliation. By engaging in interfaith dialogues, practitioners and scholars can identify these shared values and work towards a collective understanding of restorative justice.

3. Interdisciplinary Collaboration: Restorative justice is inherently interdisciplinary, drawing from fields like law, psychology, sociology, and theology. Interdisciplinary dialogues enable experts from various disciplines to collaborate and develop a holistic approach to restorative justice that considers multiple dimensions.

4. Conflict Resolution: Restorative justice is often applied in conflict resolution contexts. Interfaith and interdisciplinary dialogues can provide insights and strategies for applying these principles to manage conflicts effectively and promote peace.

5. Global Perspectives: Restorative justice has global relevance, and international perspectives are valuable. Engaging in interfaith and interdisciplinary dialogues with a global focus allows for the exchange of practices, lessons, and innovations from various parts of the world.

6. Ethical Considerations: Restorative justice is deeply rooted in ethical considerations. Interfaith dialogues can contribute to ethical discussions, helping to define common ethical principles that underpin restorative justice practices.

7. Education and Advocacy: Interfaith and interdisciplinary dialogues can play a role in educating communities and advocating for the adoption of restorative justice principles in various settings, including schools, criminal justice systems, and conflict resolution programs.

8. Practical Applications: By bringing together individuals from diverse backgrounds and disciplines, these dialogues can result in practical strategies and guidelines for implementing restorative justice in real-world situations.

9. Overcoming Misconceptions: Restorative justice may have misconceptions or biases associated with it. Interfaith and interdisciplinary dialogues can help dispel these misconceptions and foster a more accurate and informed understanding of the approach.

10. Community Building: These dialogues can promote community building and strengthen the bonds between faith communities, academics, practitioners, and policymakers, all of whom play a role in advancing restorative justice.

In essence, interfaith and interdisciplinary dialogues not only enrich the understanding of restorative justice but also offer a platform for collaboration, advocacy, and the development of practical applications. They provide a space where shared values, ethical considerations, and diverse perspectives converge to advance the cause of justice, healing, and reconciliation, as inspired

by the teachings of Romans and embraced by a global and diverse
community.

CHAPTER 12

RESTORATIVE JUSTICE AND HEALING

Restorative justice and healing are intimately connected, as restorative justice processes aim to facilitate healing for both victims and offenders. Here's how restorative justice contributes to healing:

1. Acknowledgment of Harm: Restorative justice begins by acknowledging the harm that has been done. This recognition is essential for the healing process, as it validates the pain and suffering experienced by the victim.

2. Empowerment: Restorative justice gives victims a voice, allowing them to express their feelings, concerns, and needs. This empowerment can be a crucial part of the healing journey, as victims regain a sense of control over their lives.

3. Offender Accountability: Restorative justice encourages offenders to take responsibility for their actions and the harm they've caused. This acknowledgment can be a significant step toward healing, as it validates the victim's experience.

4. Apology and Forgiveness: In many restorative justice processes, offenders offer genuine apologies to their victims. Victims, in turn, have the opportunity to forgive. This exchange can be deeply healing, allowing both parties to let go of anger and resentment.

5. Reparations and Restitution: Restorative justice often includes actions aimed at making amends, such as restitution. These actions can help repair the tangible harm caused and provide a sense of closure to victims.

6. Community Support: Restorative justice frequently involves the broader community in the process, providing a support network for victims and offenders. Community support can be instrumental in the healing journey.

7. Preventing Recidivism: By addressing the underlying issues that lead to criminal behavior, restorative justice can contribute to preventing repeat offenses, further promoting healing for victims, and reducing the potential for future harm.

8. Resolution of Trauma: For many victims, restorative justice offers a means to address and resolve trauma. The healing journey often involves a shift from being a victim to being a survivor.

9. Humanization: Restorative justice processes humanize both victims and offenders. They allow individuals to see each other as more than just the roles they've played in a criminal act, promoting empathy and understanding.

10. Personal Growth: For some offenders, participating in restorative justice processes can be a catalyst for personal growth and change. This transformation contributes to healing, not only for themselves but also for their communities.

11. Healing Circles: Restorative justice practices like healing circles provide a structured environment for participants to express their feelings and experiences. These circles can be instrumental in the healing process.

12. Catharsis and Closure: Restorative justice processes can offer catharsis, emotional release, and a sense of closure for both victims and offenders. This closure is an essential component of the healing journey.

In summary, restorative justice actively seeks to address harm and promote healing through its victim-centered, accountable, and community-engaged processes. It recognizes that healing is a multi-faceted journey that extends beyond mere retribution and punishment, seeking to restore individuals, relationships, and communities in the aftermath of harm.

CHAPTER 13

RESTORATIVE JUSTICE AND CRIMINAL JUSTICE

Restorative justice and criminal justice are two distinct approaches to addressing wrongdoing and conflicts within a society. Here's a comparison of their key principles and practices:

Criminal Justice:

1. Punitive Focus: Criminal justice systems primarily focus on punishing offenders through incarceration, fines, probation, or other punitive measures. The emphasis is on retribution and deterrence.

2. Government-Led: The state takes the central role in criminal justice processes, including investigations, prosecutions, and adjudications.

3. Adversarial: The criminal justice process is adversarial, with prosecution and defense presenting their cases in court. Outcomes are often determined by a judge or jury.

4. Victim as Witness: Victims in the criminal justice system are typically treated as witnesses to the crime, with their main role being to provide evidence for the prosecution.

5. Limited Victim Participation: Victims have limited participation in the process, and their needs and desires may not be

central to the outcome. Their primary role is to seek justice through conviction.

6. Sentencing: Sentences are typically determined by legal guidelines and statutes, with an emphasis on proportionality to the crime.

Restorative Justice:

1. Restorative Focus: Restorative justice aims to repair the harm caused by the offense. The emphasis is on reconciliation, healing, and reintegration.

2. Community-Led: Restorative justice processes often involve community members, mediators, and other stakeholders in addressing harm. The state may play a supportive role but is not the sole decision-maker.

3. Collaborative: Restorative justice processes are collaborative and involve open dialogue between victims and offenders. Outcomes are often determined through consensus.

4. Victim as Central: Victims are central to restorative justice processes, with their needs, feelings, and desires taking precedence. They have an active role in shaping the outcome.

5. Extensive Victim Participation: Victims have a significant role in the process, including the opportunity to express their feelings, ask questions, and participate in decision-making.

6. Restitution and Reintegration: Outcomes in restorative justice can include restitution, apologies, and plans for the reintegration of the offender into the community. The focus is on repairing relationships and addressing the root causes of the offense.

In summary, criminal justice emphasizes punishment and government-led processes, while restorative justice seeks to repair harm and involves collaborative, community-led approaches. The two approaches can coexist, and some justice systems integrate restorative practices as an alternative or complementary method to traditional punitive measures. Restorative justice is often seen as a way to humanize the justice system, offer healing to victims, and promote accountability and rehabilitation for offenders.

CHAPTER 14

RESTORATIVE JUSTICE IN THE GLOBAL CONTEXT

Restorative justice has gained recognition and adoption in various parts of the world, reflecting its universal appeal as an alternative approach to addressing harm, conflict, and crime. Here's how restorative justice is manifesting in the global context:

1. Different Cultural Adaptations: Restorative justice is adapted to fit the cultural contexts of various regions. Practices may vary, but the core principles of addressing harm, promoting reconciliation, and involving stakeholders remain consistent.

2. Legal Frameworks: Some countries have integrated restorative justice into their legal systems, recognizing it as a formal option within the criminal justice process. For example, New Zealand's Family Group Conferences and various European countries' victim-offender mediation programs.

3. Community-Based Initiatives: In many parts of the world, restorative justice is implemented through community-based organizations and initiatives rather than as part of the formal legal system. These organizations may address issues ranging from juvenile crime to domestic disputes.

4. Indigenous Practices: Restorative justice aligns with many indigenous justice practices. In some countries, these practices have been recognized and incorporated into the formal

justice system. For instance, Canada's restorative justice programs within indigenous communities.

5. Conflict Resolution: Restorative justice principles are applied in conflict resolution, peacebuilding, and transitional justice processes. This approach has been used in post-conflict societies to address historical injustices and promote reconciliation.

6. International Organizations: Restorative justice is promoted by international organizations like the United Nations as a means to promote reconciliation, transitional justice, and the reintegration of former combatants.

7. Human Rights Focus: Restorative justice intersects with human rights concerns, addressing issues such as the rights of victims, offenders, and marginalized populations. It has been used to promote accountability for human rights abuses and mass atrocities.

8. Cross-Border Applications: Restorative justice can cross borders in cases involving international crimes or disputes. It can facilitate reconciliation between nations and address transnational issues.

9. Victims' Rights: Restorative justice supports the rights and needs of victims, which are increasingly recognized as a global concern. Initiatives like the Declaration of Basic Principles of Justice for Victims of Crime and Abuse of Power emphasize victim-centered approaches.

10. Conflict Prevention: Restorative justice is recognized as a tool for conflict prevention by addressing underlying issues, reducing recidivism, and fostering dialogue between groups with historical tensions.

11. Community Engagement: In some regions, restorative justice is seen as a means to engage communities in addressing crime and conflicts, promoting a sense of shared responsibility for justice and healing.

In the global context, restorative justice is seen as a versatile approach that can adapt to various legal, cultural, and social settings. Its principles align with the promotion of human rights, reconciliation, and community-building, making it a valuable tool in addressing conflicts and injustices on an international scale.

Global inspiration in the context of restorative justice refers to the adoption and application of restorative justice principles in various parts of the world to address a wide range of local and global challenges. These examples demonstrate that restorative justice is not confined to one culture, region, or context but has universal relevance. Here are some illustrations of global inspiration:

1. South Africa's Truth and Reconciliation Commission: South Africa's Truth and Reconciliation Commission (TRC) is one of the most iconic examples of restorative justice on a national scale. The TRC aimed to address the historical injustices of apartheid by providing a platform for victims and perpetrators to share their stories and seek reconciliation. It served as an inspiration for truth and reconciliation processes in other post-conflict societies.

2. Canada's Indigenous Healing Circles: In Canada, Indigenous communities have adopted the principles of restorative justice in the form of healing circles. These circles provide opportunities for dialogue, healing, and reconciliation, particularly in addressing historical injustices against Indigenous peoples. This approach has gained recognition and inspired similar initiatives globally.

3. Rwanda's Gacaca Courts: In the aftermath of the Rwandan genocide, the country established Gacaca courts as a form of community-based justice. These courts incorporated elements of restorative justice by encouraging perpetrators to confess their crimes and seek reconciliation with their victims. The Gacaca process served as an inspiration for transitional justice initiatives in other post-conflict regions.

4. Scandinavian Criminal Justice Systems: Countries like Norway, Sweden, and Finland have integrated restorative justice principles into their criminal justice systems. These systems focus on rehabilitation, reconciliation, and reintegration, rather than punitive measures. Their success in reducing recidivism rates has inspired criminal justice reforms in other parts of the world.

5. New Zealand's Restorative Justice Practices: New Zealand has widely embraced restorative justice practices, particularly within its youth justice system. These practices involve victims, offenders, and the community in finding solutions that repair harm and promote accountability. Other countries have

looked to New Zealand's approach as a model for juvenile justice reform.

6. Victims of Crime Support Groups: Support groups for victims of crime, which incorporate restorative justice principles, have emerged in various countries. These groups offer victims opportunities to share their experiences, find support, and seek healing. They draw inspiration from the idea that victims' voices should be heard and their needs addressed.

7. Community Policing Initiatives: Some communities around the world have adopted community policing models that emphasize restorative approaches to address conflicts and build trust between law enforcement and the community. These models have inspired innovative law enforcement practices in different regions.

8. Interfaith Peace and Reconciliation Initiatives: In regions marked by religious or ethnic conflicts, interfaith peace and reconciliation initiatives have embraced restorative justice principles. These efforts seek to bridge divides, promote dialogue, and facilitate reconciliation among different communities.

9. United Nations and International Efforts: The United Nations and international organizations have recognized the importance of restorative justice in various contexts, such as post-conflict peacebuilding and transitional justice. These global efforts acknowledge the universal relevance of restorative principles.

10. Non-Governmental Organizations: Numerous non-governmental organizations (NGOs) worldwide work to promote restorative justice principles in various areas, including criminal justice, education, and conflict resolution. Their initiatives serve as global inspirations for grassroots restorative justice advocacy.

In summary, these global examples of restorative justice initiatives underscore the universal relevance of restorative principles in addressing a wide range of local and global challenges. They demonstrate the adaptability and effectiveness of restorative justice in various cultural, social, and political contexts and serve as inspirations for similar efforts around the world.

The vision for a restorative society is one where the principles of restorative justice are not merely an option but an integral way of life. It's a society that values healing over harm, understanding over judgment, and reconciliation over retribution. In this vision:

The default response to harm is healing. Instead of punitive measures that perpetuate cycles of violence and retribution, a restorative society prioritizes the recovery and well-being of all its members. Victims are supported, offenders are held accountable, and communities mend.

A restorative society holds individuals accountable for their actions and encourages them to take responsibility for their wrongdoings. It recognizes that accountability is not about punishment but about making amends and learning from one's mistakes.

Empathy and understanding are the cornerstones of this society. People actively listen to one another, seeking to understand each other's perspectives, experiences, and needs. This understanding fosters compassion and promotes unity.

Reconciliation is the ultimate goal, even in the face of deep conflicts. Communities strive to rebuild trust through dialogue and acknowledgment of past wrongs. They understand that true reconciliation takes time but is worth the effort.

A restorative society places a strong emphasis on preventing harm. It invests in conflict resolution skills, education, and community-building initiatives to proactively address potential conflicts before they escalate.

Restorative justice is woven into the educational system, teaching the next generation the principles of healing, accountability, and reconciliation. Young minds grow up with an understanding of restorative values.

Communities play an active role in addressing conflicts and promoting healing. Neighborhoods, schools, workplaces, and faith communities are equipped with the tools and training to facilitate dialogue and reconciliation.

The criminal justice system undergoes a fundamental shift. Prisons are transformed into places of rehabilitation, where offenders are given opportunities for personal growth and transformation. Recidivism rates decrease significantly.

The principles of restorative justice from the Book of Romans serve as a source of inspiration not only within communities but also on a global scale. Nations come together to address international conflicts with the values of reconciliation, understanding, and healing.

A restorative society embraces diversity, recognizing that every individual has inherent worth and dignity. It actively addresses systemic inequalities, working to dismantle oppressive structures.

Restorative practices are employed in various sectors, including family, schools, workplaces, and international diplomacy. Conflicts are resolved with the goal of healing and preserving relationships.

Interfaith and interdisciplinary dialogues thrive, promoting shared values of justice, healing, and reconciliation. Collaboration across diverse faiths, disciplines, and cultures enriches the society's capacity to address complex issues.

In this vision for a restorative society, the ongoing work of individuals, communities, and institutions is paramount. It's an acknowledgment that the transformation to a restorative way of life is a journey, requiring dedication and effort. But the potential for positive change in the lives of individuals, families, and communities is profound. It's a vision worth pursuing—one where reconciliation, understanding, and healing are at the heart of our shared human experience.

CHAPTER 15

RESTORATIVE JUSTICE IN EDUCATION

Restorative justice in education is an approach that focuses on building and maintaining positive relationships within school communities while addressing conflicts and misconduct. It has gained popularity as a means to create a more inclusive and supportive learning environment. Here's how restorative justice is applied in education:

1. Conflict Resolution: Restorative justice practices are used to address conflicts, disputes, and disciplinary issues within schools. Rather than punitive measures, these processes promote dialogue and understanding.

2. Empathy and Communication: Students are encouraged to develop empathy and communication skills. Restorative justice circles and discussions help students express themselves, listen to others, and build relationships.

3. Peer Mediation: Many schools implement peer mediation programs, where trained student mediators assist their peers in resolving conflicts. This approach empowers students to take an active role in addressing issues.

4. Community Building: Restorative justice activities, such as circles, are used to build a sense of community within schools. These circles encourage trust, respect, and a feeling of belonging among students and staff.

5. Disciplinary Alternatives: Restorative practices provide alternatives to traditional disciplinary actions. Students who engage in wrongdoing are encouraged to take responsibility, make amends, and learn from their actions.

6. Victim-Centered: Restorative justice in education is victim-centered, focusing on the needs and perspectives of those harmed. Victims are allowed to share their experiences and influence the resolution process.

7. Accountability and Responsibility: Offenders are held accountable for their actions and encouraged to take responsibility. This can involve actions like apologizing to the victim, performing community service, or making restitution.

8. Reduction in Suspensions and Expulsions: Restorative justice can lead to a reduction in suspensions and expulsions by addressing the root causes of problematic behavior and promoting student understanding and growth.

9. Prevention of Bullying: Restorative justice programs can be instrumental in preventing and addressing bullying. They create a safe space for victims and offenders to discuss their experiences and work toward resolution.

10. Positive School Climate: Restorative justice practices contribute to a positive school climate where students, teachers, and staff feel respected, heard, and supported. This, in turn, can improve academic performance and overall well-being.

11. Reintegration: Restorative justice helps reintegrate students who have been involved in wrongdoing back into the school community, promoting growth and learning from their mistakes.

12. Life Skills: Restorative practices teach life skills such as conflict resolution, effective communication, and empathy, which are valuable not only in school but also in students' future lives.

Restorative justice in education aims to foster a culture of respect, accountability, and empathy within schools. It promotes positive relationships, supports student development, and offers a more effective approach to addressing behavioral issues compared to punitive measures.

CHAPTER 16

RESTORATIVE JUSTICE IN FAMILY RELATIONSHIP

Restorative justice principles and practices can be applied in family and relationship contexts to address conflicts, heal emotional wounds, and rebuild trust. Here's how restorative justice is used in family and relationship settings:

1. Conflict Resolution: Restorative justice offers a structured approach for resolving conflicts within families and relationships. This process encourages open communication, empathy, and understanding between parties.

2. Dialogue and Communication: Restorative justice practices promote healthy dialogue and communication. Family members or partners have the opportunity to express their feelings, listen to each other, and find common ground.

3. Rebuilding Trust: In cases of betrayal or harm within a family or relationship, restorative justice can be a tool for rebuilding trust. Offenders can acknowledge their wrongdoing and work toward making amends.

4. Accountability and Responsibility: Restorative justice encourages individuals to take responsibility for their actions. This can involve acknowledging the harm caused and taking steps to rectify it.

5. Apology and Forgiveness: Apologies are a central part of restorative justice. Offenders may offer sincere apologies, and

victims are given the opportunity to forgive. This process can be deeply healing.

6. Family Meetings: Restorative justice may involve family meetings or conferences where all members come together to discuss issues, reach resolutions, and work on healing relationships.

7. Victim-Centered: Restorative justice places the needs and experiences of victims at the forefront. It allows victims to have a voice, express their emotions, and actively participate in the resolution process.

8. Long-Term Healing: The focus is not merely on addressing immediate conflicts but on promoting long-term healing and understanding within families and relationships.

9. Prevention: Restorative justice practices can help prevent further harm by addressing the root causes of conflicts, reducing tension, and improving communication.

10. Empathy and Understanding: Participants are encouraged to develop empathy and understanding for each other's perspectives, which can be transformative in rebuilding relationships.

11. Resolution of Family Disputes: In family settings, restorative justice can be used to address a wide range of disputes, including conflicts between parents and children, sibling rivalry, and issues related to inheritance or family property.

12. Couples Therapy: Restorative justice principles are integrated into couples therapy and relationship counseling to facilitate healthy conflict resolution and relationship repair.

13. Child Welfare: Restorative justice practices can be used in child welfare cases to address issues related to neglect, abuse, or parental disputes, with a focus on ensuring the child's well-being.

Applying restorative justice within families and relationships fosters a culture of empathy, accountability, and reconciliation. It helps individuals address underlying issues, heal emotional wounds, and build stronger, more supportive, and healthier connections.

CHAPTER 17

CASE STUDIES IN RESTORATIVE JUSTICE

Case studies in restorative justice offer practical examples of how this approach has been applied in various contexts. Here are a few case studies illustrating the use of restorative justice principles and practices:

1. Victim-Offender Mediation in Germany: Germany has a well-established system of victim-offender mediation. In one case, a teenage offender who had committed a property crime was brought into mediation with the victim. Through this process, the offender not only returned the stolen items but also understood the impact of his actions on the victim. The victim, in turn, found closure and forgave the offender. Research has shown a significant reduction in recidivism rates for offenders who participated in such mediation.

2. Maori Restorative Justice in New Zealand: New Zealand has integrated Maori restorative justice practices into its legal system. These practices, known as Family Group Conferences (FGCs), allow the victim, offender, and their families to come together and discuss offenses. In one case, an FGC was used to address a youth's burglary of a family's home. The FGC allowed for open communication and a focus on healing and reintegration, which is central to Maori cultural values.

3. Restorative Circles in Schools: Restorative circles are widely used in schools to address conflicts and behavioral issues. In a case study, a high school used restorative circles to address bullying and conflicts among students. These circles provided a safe space for students to share their experiences and perspectives, leading to increased empathy and a reduction in bullying incidents.

4. Restorative Justice in the Criminal Justice System - Belgium: Belgium has incorporated restorative justice into its legal system, particularly for certain juvenile cases. In one case, a young offender who had committed a theft was brought into a restorative justice process involving the victim. Through dialogue and reparation, the victim felt heard and the offender gained insight into the consequences of his actions. The victim was compensated, and the offender was less likely to re-offend.

5. Truth and Reconciliation Commission in South Africa: While not purely a restorative justice process, the Truth and Reconciliation Commission (TRC) in South Africa allowed for the open discussion of human rights abuses and reconciliation between victims and perpetrators. The TRC played a significant role in addressing the legacy of apartheid and promoting healing and reconciliation.

These case studies demonstrate the versatility and effectiveness of restorative justice in addressing a wide range of conflicts and offenses. Whether applied in criminal justice, schools, or cultural contexts, restorative justice processes have the potential to promote healing, reconciliation, and accountability while reducing recidivism and harm.

CHAPTER 18

RESTORATIVE JUSTICE AND THEOLOGY

Restorative justice and theology share common principles and values, making them closely intertwined in certain theological perspectives. Here's how restorative justice aligns with theological principles:

1. Redemption and Forgiveness: Many theological traditions, including Christianity, emphasize the concepts of redemption and forgiveness. Restorative justice embodies these principles by providing opportunities for offenders to make amends, seek forgiveness, and ultimately redeem themselves in the eyes of both human society and the divine.

2. Reconciliation: Theological teachings often highlight reconciliation as a fundamental aspect of faith. Restorative justice actively promotes reconciliation, both between individuals and with the divine, in the context of conflicts and wrongdoing.

3. Community and Restoration: Restorative justice emphasizes the importance of community involvement and support in the justice process. This aligns with the theological concept of community and the role it plays in providing moral guidance, forgiveness, and healing.

4. Accountability: The idea of moral accountability is central to many theological systems. Restorative justice holds offenders accountable for their actions while offering them a path

to redemption, reflecting the theological belief in individual responsibility and accountability.

5. Healing and Transformation: Both restorative justice and theology share a focus on healing and personal transformation. These approaches recognize that offenders can change, grow, and seek a more righteous path.

6. Non-Retaliation: Some theological teachings, such as the "turn the other cheek" principle in Christianity, emphasize non-retaliation and the pursuit of peace. Restorative justice aligns with these values by seeking non-punitive resolutions.

7. Justice as Love: In some theological perspectives, justice is seen as an expression of divine love. Restorative justice embodies this concept by emphasizing love, empathy, and care in the process of addressing harm.

8. Empathy and Compassion: Theological principles often stress the importance of empathy and compassion for others. Restorative justice encourages participants to empathize with one another and to approach conflicts with a compassionate mindset.

9. Liberation Theology: Liberation theology, which focuses on social justice and the marginalized, has strong connections with restorative justice. Both approaches seek to address social inequalities and injustices, promoting healing and liberation.

10. Sacrificial Love: The concept of sacrificial love is present in many theological traditions. Restorative justice allows individuals to make amends for their wrongdoing, which can be seen as a form of sacrificial love in action.

It's important to note that while restorative justice aligns with these theological principles, not all theological perspectives are in complete agreement with this approach. Some theological views emphasize retribution and punishment as more appropriate forms of justice. However, for those who find resonance in the principles of redemption, reconciliation, and healing, restorative justice offers a framework that complements and embodies their theological values.

CHAPTER 19

FUTURE DIRECTIONS AND CHALLENGES

The future of restorative justice holds promise as well as challenges as it continues to evolve and expand. Here are some future directions and challenges for restorative justice:

Future Directions:

1. Integration with Mainstream Justice Systems: One future direction is the continued integration of restorative justice into mainstream justice systems. This includes expanding its use in criminal justice, family law, and other areas of the legal system.

2. Global Expansion: Restorative justice is likely to continue its global expansion, adapting to different cultural contexts and legal systems. International organizations and governments are increasingly recognizing its value in promoting reconciliation and addressing harm.

3. Research and Evaluation: Future directions include more robust research and evaluation of restorative justice programs. Gathering evidence of their effectiveness can help inform policy decisions and improve practices.

4. Prevention and Early Intervention: Restorative justice can be applied as a preventive tool. Future efforts may focus on early intervention and the use of restorative practices to address conflicts and wrongdoing before they escalate.

5. Restorative Practices in Education: The use of restorative practices in education is expected to grow. Schools are recognizing the benefits of creating a more inclusive, empathetic, and accountable learning environment.

6. Community-Led Initiatives: The future may see an expansion of community-led restorative justice initiatives that empower communities to address conflicts and harm on their terms.

7. Technology Integration: The use of technology, such as virtual conferencing and digital tools, may expand the reach of restorative justice processes, making them more accessible and efficient.

Challenges:

1. Resistance from Traditional Systems: One of the primary challenges is resistance from traditional justice systems that may view restorative justice as a threat to established punitive practices.

2. Quality Assurance: Ensuring the quality and consistency of restorative justice programs and processes is a challenge. Proper training and adherence to best practices are essential.

3. Victim and Offender Safety: Balancing the needs for victim and offender safety while conducting face-to-face meetings in restorative processes can be a challenge in some cases.

4. Equity and Access: Ensuring equitable access to restorative justice processes and addressing disparities in participation is a challenge that requires ongoing attention.

5. Funding and Resources: Restorative justice programs often struggle with limited funding and resources, hindering their ability to reach their full potential.

6. Cultural Sensitivity: Adapting restorative justice to diverse cultural contexts and ensuring cultural sensitivity is a challenge, as approaches may need to be customized to fit local norms and values.

7. Public Perception: Overcoming public skepticism or misconceptions about restorative justice can be challenging, especially when it's seen as too lenient or an alternative to traditional punishment.

8. Complex Cases: Certain complex cases, such as those involving severe violence or mass atrocities, pose challenges for restorative justice processes.

Addressing these challenges and pursuing the future directions of restorative justice requires a concerted effort from policymakers, practitioners, communities, and stakeholders. It involves refining and improving practices, promoting awareness, and advocating for the values of reconciliation, healing, and accountability that restorative justice represents.

EMBRACING RESTORATIVE JUSTICE THROUGH THE LENS OF JESUS

In conclusion, embracing restorative justice through the lens of Jesus provides a profound and transformative perspective on how we can approach conflict, harm, and justice. The teachings and life of Jesus, as recorded in the Gospels, offer a compelling foundation for the principles and practices of restorative justice. Through the lens of Jesus, we find a vision of justice rooted in love, compassion, forgiveness, reconciliation, and the restoration of individuals and communities.

The alignment between Jesus' teachings and restorative justice is striking. His emphasis on compassion, mercy, and the intrinsic worth of every person aligns perfectly with the principles of understanding, empathy, and respect that underpin restorative justice.

Key elements of Jesus' teachings, such as forgiveness and reconciliation, lie at the heart of restorative justice processes. His parables and actions highlight the power of storytelling, dialogue, and community involvement, all central elements of restorative justice.

Jesus' model of justice as love in action reflects the restorative justice approach that aims to address harm with love, empathy, and care, not retribution and punishment.

By embracing restorative justice through the lens of Jesus, we are inspired to approach conflicts and harm with the same values and principles that he embodied. This approach invites us to seek healing and transformation, to acknowledge the dignity of all individuals, to promote accountability, and to work toward the reconciliation of broken relationships.

In a world where punitive justice systems often prevail, the lens of Jesus encourages us to embrace restorative justice as a path that can lead us to a more compassionate, empathetic, and reconciled society. As we journey forward, we are reminded that the principles of restorative justice are not only an effective means to address harm but also a profound embodiment of love and justice in action, as exemplified by the life and teachings of Jesus.

www.ingramcontent.com/pod-product-compliance
Lightning Source LLC
Chambersburg PA
CBHW061254120726
48001CB00001B/296